# Praise for Sofia

"Sofia is the epitome of Triumph over adversity. Her courage and warmth is such an inspiration to all. I feel honored to be her Facebook friend."-

"Sofia is one of the sweetest, Lovin, Honest folk I know. She does not let things keep her down for long. She always has a family or friends back as long as they are in the right. I love ya Lots GF." -

"Sofia and I have been friends for a long time and she's been through a lot in life. She's here to help others in their lives with understanding, good advice about abuse because she's been through it. She cares deeply for others and will willingly walk you through the storm as much as she can." -

"Sofia, who I have nicknamed has helped me in so many ways. the most important one is helping me to remember I need to be myself and love myself for who I am and what I have been through." -

"I've known Sofia James for almost 30 years. During that time I have come to feel like she is my sister. We have been through so much together and we have always had each other's back. This is a treasure in both of our lives. In the times that I have witnessed her adversities, she has always risen to the top. all the while inspiring others to do the same." -

"In the short time I have known Sofia she has always been a light at the end of a Darkened tunnel. Her light shines through in everything she does. She has a warm heart and loves everyone. She is very easy to talk to and brings joy to everyone she meets. Some of us who have gotten close to her have nicknamed her, because of the Joy she brings to every situation." -

"Faced with a myriad of trials and tribulations throughout her life, Sofia James has refused to allow those experiences to define her. Instead, she has made it her mission to share her invaluable insight with the sea of others who may be suffering insurmountable torment, be it at the hands of others or self- imposed, through her increasingly popular videos on social media. Now with the release of her much-anticipated autobiography, her devoted fans are allowed a glimpse into the events that lead her down the path she was destined for."-

*Theresa*

# Taking
## a Different
# Path

*Finding Joy in the Journey*

*Thank You*

SOFIA JAMES

*Sofia James*

WESTBOW
PRESS®
A DIVISION OF THOMAS NELSON
& ZONDERVAN

*Joeann Hall Crafton*

*FB*

WestBow Press books may be ordered through booksellers or by contacting:

WestBow Press
A Division of Thomas Nelson & Zondervan
1663 Liberty Drive
Bloomington, IN 47403
www.westbowpress.com
844-714-3454

Scripture quotations taken from The Holy Bible, New International Version® NIV® Copyright © 1973 1978 1984 2011 by Biblica, Inc. TM. Used by permission. All rights reserved worldwide.

Scripture taken from the King James Version of the Bible.

ISBN: 978-1-6642-3636-3 (sc)
ISBN: 978-1-6642-3635-6 (e)

Print information available on the last page.

WestBow Press rev. date: 7/28/2021

This book is dedicated to
"The Warrior in Every One of Us"

# Contents

# *Introduction*

In everyone's life we have been judged, either falsely or correctly. I have been judged many times. Fortunately, I am a strong woman. I have had my times of doubt, but that still small voice in my head would tell me the truth in a personal way and it would always steer me in the right direction. It would tell me to bravely keep placing one foot in front of the other, sometimes blindly, but at all times be led by Jesus knowing He has me safely in his hands.

Throughout my life I have kept one thing intact, my sense of humor! This I acquired from my daddy and my uncle! My sense of humor and the Lord have helped me through the hard things in my life. He (the Lord) still does to this day.

My dad and uncle were always taking a popular song and changing the words to make it funny. This was hilarious. My mother would always say, "If you can't sing the song correctly, then don't sing it at all." I would always tell my dad and uncle to, "Sing it again! Sing it again!"

The things I have been through will never define who I am, but they are an integral part of me. These things have made me who I am today! I have a rich heritage that includes grandparents and great grandparents, many aunts, uncles and others who have stepped in and helped shape me into who I am. I have loving friends and a few relatives who have invested into my life, including a longstanding babysitter who was also a neighbor. I have always felt loved by these people because they invested in me and pushed me to do better. I realized as I got older that it was because they cared for, loved and believed that there were hidden talents and abilities that I was not utilizing. They had faith in me and I now pay it forward and pass on this same ability to others as a result of these people.

I love my family, but I never felt like I fit in. I always would daydream that I was an alien and that my ship was coming to get me at any time. I would dream that I was adopted and that someone would tell me the truth so I could go search for my "real" family. It also came to my mind that I had a twin who was exactly like me who would love, accept and understand me unconditionally. Unfortunately, funny and sadly, none of those things ever happened!

Here I am at fifty-seven writing a book! It is a story of strength, growth, change and overcoming issues that I have dealt with since childhood.

I would like to say that writing this book has been therapeutic as this is my fifth revision, and it is finally near printing.

At first, when I began writing this book, I was filled with anger and hatred towards those who hurt, used, abused and failed to protect me. God said to remove all the feelings of blame, shame, guilt and hatred. Now this journey is different. Taking this different path means change of epic proportions. It means telling the truth even though my family has always told me to stay quiet and keep the "family secret". Secrets are far too heavy a burden to keep and carry. So instead I became a storyteller. This also means doing things differently and NOT repeating things that I disliked that were done to me as a child. As a result of the abuse I suffered at the hands of my parents I chose to change how I treated, corrected and disciplined my children. This is something that no child should ever have to face. This included being brave, honest and true to myself even though I was told to, "Shut up", "Don't get involved", "Stay invisible" and "Stay silent". This was not me, how I felt or believed and those statements never sat well internally. Through this, I have been true and authentic to myself and for myself. I am breaking generational curses and overcoming obstacles.

*"May we discover through pain and torment,*
*the strength to live with grace and humor.*
*May we discover through doubt and anguish,*
*the strength to live with dignity and holiness.*
*May we discover through suffering and fear,*
*the strength to move toward healing.*
*May it come to pass that we be restored to health and to vigor.*
*May life grant us wellness of body, spirit, and mind.*
*And if this cannot be so, may we find in this transformation and passage*
*moments of meaning, opportunities for love*
*and the deep and gracious calm that comes*
*when we allow ourselves to move on."*

———

RABBI RAMI M. SHAPIRO

# 1

⟡

*Tarnished Treasure*

*"Basically, Aristotle believed that every time you behaved
unkind and immorally-performing actions your soul was
not proud of-you tarnished your soul. The worst shape your
soul became, the worst shape your mood and spirit."*

**KAREN SALMANSOHN**

---

I CAME INTO THIS WORLD ON a cold winter morning. I am the oldest of children born to my parents. My life pretty much started at five, as I do not remember much prior to this time. Perhaps it is the trauma of abuse that took over everything I might have known or remembered.

At five I was molested by a male friend of the family who was given permission to babysit. He took me into another bedroom of the house we lived in and said, "If you don't let me do what I want to do to you, I am gonna do it to someone else." What choice did I have? My job as the oldest child is to protect, right?

Somewhere between five and eleven another male family friend became entrusted to "babysit" and he also began molesting me. Mom and dad would go bowling at night as dad was in a league. They would hire anyone so they could go. I would ask, "Who is babysitting tonight?" If I would hear two specific names then I would cry out, "No, not them! Please! Someone else!" This was to no avail.

**"About 90% of children who are victims of abuse know their abuser. About 60% of children who are sexually abused are abused by the people the family trusts." (Darkness to Light, "Child Sexual Abuse Statistics, Perpentrators", d2l.org)**

We moved into the city when I was eleven, others started molesting me as well. These were male friends of the family. Some of these "friends of the family" used the guise that I was their girlfriend. They would "feel me up" and tell me I looked "pretty". Though none of them had sex with me. It left me feeling ashamed, dirty, used and ruined.

The things I do remember as being good and worthwhile were baseball, riding my bike and swimming during the summer. I loved it. I loved doing anything with my grandparents and great grandparents. Often this included camping with the great grandparents and grandparents. I would go down to the pool or lake and swim and jump off the dock. There was a pontoon on the lake that you could swim to and the lake was crystal clear and you can see to the bottom. I find this so amazingly beautiful, serene and also comforting.

I guess I was never meant to be normal. But, from what I heard, normal is only a setting on your dryer.

Dad was abusive and mom was in her own little world. My dad would point and "doink" at my forehead and upper chest/breast bone in anger or while he was yelling or screaming. He would do this while he was in a rage. I know they both tried to do better then what was done for them and in some instances they succeeded. Though there were far more instances in which they did not.

As I grew older, I read books and heard so many stories of kids whose parents were much more severe and abusive than mine. I had heard some stories of kids who were burned, beaten, locked in closets, starved and worse. There was always someone else worse off than I had it.

I am estranged from my siblings at the time of the writing of this book, and I do not see this changing anytime soon. I have survived losing both parents and now I feel as though I am an orphan. They say death brings out the worst in people and I know this to be true. God knows what has happened and I will let him be the judge and vindicator!

While growing up I always felt they were all in the same "bubble" and I was the outsider. I was the "black sheep" of the family. It seems it has always been this way.

It came to my attention later-on in life that there was a fire in the travel trailer where my parents and I lived when I was a small baby. Apparently, when it was on fire, my mother ran out without me, then my dad ran back into the trailer to save me. The fire was near the end of my crib. I was so thankful that my dad was there to rescue me or I might not have survived.

As a child I felt I did not get the education that I needed and I was bored all the time. I read four pages a day in the dictionary and then challenged myself to use one of the words in a sentence the next day. I also made-up stories with "the girls" (aka my breasts) about others or situations we saw. We would laugh and at least it brought humor into my life. I thought about making a comic book about our adventures.

When I was older (twelve to fifteen) I tried to talk to friends about what happened to me as a child but found only judgement, disbelief and blame as though I was responsible for what had happened to me. I was fortunate to have an inner voice that at first quietly said, "You were victimized, and this treatment is wrong".

As time went by this voice kept getting louder and louder in my head. Before long I grew to trust this voice, knowing it knew and served me better than anyone.

I quit talking to friends about what had happened to me and only talked to my stuffed animals. I was tired of the shame, guilt and blame. My stuffed animals were my friend and would never judge, hurt, betray or use what I had said against me. I also quit writing poetry as I was afraid that the writings would be found. This was my only way of letting out my feelings. These poems spoke of how lonely I was, how awful I felt and released a lot of pent up rage and anger. But they were so dark that I worried that they would hurt people if they were found and read. It helped to put my feelings to paper.

When you have been abused, it is so hard to trust and let people in and believe that people are good. As hard as It may be to believe, I still believe that there is good in people.

Unfortunately, many who have suffered have closed themselves off just like I did for so long. Again, how lonely was I?

This was a self-imposed cave also known as prison that I had built to keep me safe and to keep others from hurting me. I was in a cave. It was dark, cold and isolated. If you could imagine a labyrinth, covered in moss with myself in the center. You had to go through the labyrinth or maze to get to me, or, for myself to get out. This was how I was protecting myself. In Maryhill, Washington, there is a copy of Stonehenge with the huge vertical stones. Imagine this on steroids with many more walls.

It did not hurt. It could not. I had closed off all my feelings. I thought that I did not and could not care anymore. This was a coping mechanism, but really it was a lie. I was hurting, but in a different way.

I made it through most of my childhood in a capped up silent world of my own where it was me against the world. Music, imagination, my stuffed animals and inner voice were my main companions. I would write poems, stories and daydreams. I would not write personal poetry. I would write poems that I was not afraid of people finding. I also played with my barbie dolls and dreamed of a much better life than I had both presently and for my future.

I would dream of torturing and killing the two men who hurt me. I was angry and lived to seek revenge.

There was a huge open sore inside me that I kept open to use as a reason to keep living. This anger served a purpose for a long time. It was my fuel for life, the reason I got up every morning. All the while I dreamt of ways to end my life, but I was too chicken to pursue any of them.

I did attempt to take my life two times by slitting my wrists. Both attempts failed and I was found by an aunt. I now know that I was meant to have my attempts fail as I have a mission and my time is not up! Most days I still feel I do not know what that mission is! Maybe, just maybe my mission is to tell my story. This story, the story of my life as I see and live it. I now know that is a huge part of my mission. to share, to encourage, show others that you can heal, grow, learn and enjoy life. A life filled with joy, happiness and a beautiful future. This is MY story.

"The majority and teen victims know the perpetrator. Of the sexual abuse cases reported to law enforcement, 93% of the juvenile victims knew the perpetrator. 59% were acquaintances, 34% were family members, 7% were strangers to the victim". (www.RAINN.org, Rape Abuse and Incest National Network).

If there is one thing that I've never heard enough of on this journey, so let me say this, "You have a right to feel hurt, used, abused, neglected, angry and whatever other feelings go with it. Your feelings are valid! But it is truly up to you and me whether we stay bitter, hurt and wounded or get BETTER! Can you say that with me? My feelings are valid, but IT IS UP TO ME TO CHOOSE BITTERNESS OR HAPPINESS!

---

Matthew 6:19 - "Lay not up for yourselves treasures upon earth, where moth and rust doth corrupt, and where thieves break through and steal."

---

# 2

⟡

## *Wounded Angel*

*"There is always tension between the possibilities we aspire to and our wounded memories and past mistakes."*

SEAN BRADY

WHEN I WAS ELEVEN I found out some people I loved and cared deeply about were being raped and molested. Because I knew how it felt to be molested I could not ignore what I was being told. I knew it to be true as the same person had attempted to molest me as well.

When I got home, I talked to my mom who immediately took me to my grandmothers. My grandmother said it was being taken care of, but I could not see any change.

For a year, I kept hearing that they could not handle the abuse and rape any longer. I no longer believed that my grandmother had reported the abuse and I knew what I had to do. The weight of what I was doing and carrying knocked me to my knees several times on the walk down to the police station. My aunt and cousin helped me up, asking If I was sure that this was what I wanted to do. I responded with a resounding, "Yes, Yes!" I had to do this. It was something I wished someone would have done to protect me all those years ago.

From the police station, after telling what I knew, I was taken in a cruiser while another cruiser followed to the house where this person was staying.

The officers went to the door and when I saw the perpetrator I was asked to identify that person. They cuffed and placed the offender in the cruiser behind us. Then they removed the children and put them in the cruiser with me. I felt so bad because I knew that it would be obvious that I was the one who came forward even though I was told not to say anything. However, I knew in my heart of hearts that I could not let this continue or carry it myself any longer! This was a huge weight for such a young girl to carry.

I had to testify in court regarding what I had heard from the defendants and what I knew personally. It was intimidating and scary, but I felt a huge urge to tell the truth. To help others in the way I was not helped as a child.

The prosecuting attorney found out that I had been molested before and tried to use it against me in court. They stated that the only reason that these allegations were made is because I hated men and had been molested by them. It was very humiliating, however worth every moment to know that I had stopped it from continuing in my family. Unfortunately, it did not stop, but it did deter it.

My aunt later went to the church where we were all attending to ask for bail money. Shockingly, they bailed the offender out! The pastor then had the gall to preach to me about forgiveness. After leaving that church we found out through the media that the pastors were involved in extramarital affairs. It was a mess. No wonder they were so "forgiving". It is not that I do not believe in forgiveness, I do. But I do not believe in assisting and ignoring abuse or burying problems.

My aunt was angry and lied to the whole family telling them I was a drug addict and that I sold my body for drugs. I felt shunned by my whole family. I also felt remorse that the children went into foster care. I have never felt one ounce of regret that I attempted to stop the abuse that was happening. Looking back though I seriously wished that my parents would have praised me for my bravery, but sadly that never happened, even worse it was never spoken about again in our home. No matter though, because I will always be proud of myself. That brave little girl just trying to do something for others that she wished someone had done for her.

I can remember thinking how blessed that I was that I didn't live with any of my offenders. It was bad enough seeing them at family gatherings always hiding behind his sunglasses.

Because I wanted love and affection from a boy, I started becoming anorexic. One day, someone walked into my room uninvited, screamed and suddenly dropped all the jars they were carrying to put into the storage area behind my room. They ran upstairs and told my mother what was seen. All mom could say was, "Look at you". She asked me what I was doing when this person entered the room. I said I was looking at myself in the mirror. Mom told me to lift-up my shirt. So, I did, and mom sucked in her breath and proceeded to get me a doctor's appointment as soon as possible. I had lost so much weight that my hips jutted out and my stomach caved in and my breasts were like empty bags hanging down in front of my body.

When we got to my appointment, I had no idea how serious my predicament was. I just wanted to be skinny so some guy would love me! That is what I thought a boyfriend wanted a skinny and pretty girlfriend. I thought that I could not be loved unless I was skinny. That is what society taught me to believe.

When my childhood doctor entered the room, he was furious. He had read my chart and the reason for my visit. We were nose to nose and he said in a barely controlled whisper, "I am giving you a week to gain weight. If you come back here next week and you have lost weight, I will slap you into the hospital in a straitjacket and feed you intravenously until you are as plump as a Christmas turkey. Ya hear me?" He was so angry! I remember this as if it was yesterday.

We left this appointment and mother and an aunt watched me night and day. I was not allowed to be in my bedroom alone because I would vomit into the sink in the laundry room.

I do not remember going back to the second appointment. Maybe I never did. The only image in my head was the image that came from others who told me how skinny I was. I was 98 pounds, stomach caved in as well as between my hips. My breasts were flat pieces of skin hanging down my chest and stomach. I thought I was beautiful! That is the result of a mind deprived of food and water.

Much later in life I turned to food and what the doctor had said came true, I was as plump as a Christmas turkey! You would never believe that I had been so thin to see me now.

During this time, I began taking care of a girl. This is a girl who was in a difficult situation. She was the daughter of some of my parent's friends. I basically adopted her starting at the age of twelve. This was when I was working two jobs. I would pick her up after school, feed her dinner, take her home, bathe her and tuck her into bed. I would pick her up in the morning and do it all over again. On the weekends she would stay with me. She and her siblings were being molested by a male family friend who "babysat" them also. I found out that her parents were being "paid" for the services he received while the parents were out on date nights. I turned him in, testified at his trial and he was put behind bars. He vowed in court that he would come to find me when he got out. He never has and he lived less than a mile away from me when I was growing up.

I sometimes cleaned houses and babysat to make money. One of the men I worked for decided that he wanted "more" from our relationship than just cleaning his house. I started to have this "check in my spirit" that there was something off with this guy. These feelings have been correct so many times.

One time I brought a family member to work with me and this man continued to corner me in the bathrooms and bedrooms. Nothing seemed to deter him so eventually I decided not to work for him any longer. I can still remember his face and the house he lived in. I learned to trust that feeling inside me. To this day I occasionally get this "check in my spirit" sometimes when I meet new people.

I started using drugs and alcohol as a coping mechanism with all I had been through. I made a little bit of money by sampling and testing pills that I received from people that I knew who I associated with. I would get a bag of pills and I would tape a pill to a sheet of paper then take this pill and describe how it made me feel and whether it was an upper or a downer. This information was used to determine how the pills were sold.

Some people that I provided babysitting services for gave me drugs and alcohol for a while. I had a friend whose boyfriend was a coke dealer. We got all the coke we wanted if she went out and rolled with him in his van. One time I blacked out when we were using coke and started to drink champagne. It was after this that I found out I was pregnant, and I quit everything cold turkey.

---

Psalms 109:22 - "For I am poor and needy, and my heart is wounded within me."

---

# 3

*A New Life*

*"If you're a good choice maker, you can choose the best emotional*
*responses and choose the best new life paths, forward and upward."*

**KAREN SALMANSOHN**

A T SIXTEEN I BECAME PREGNANT with my first child. My high school
sweetheart had left me saying that the baby was not his. I was scared
and worried about how I would take care of a child. In truth, I have been
doing so in one way or another since I was five and officially so at twelve.
So, I plunged forward knowing somehow, we would be ok!

When I was seventeen my first son was born.

Eleven months later my second son was born. When my second son
was nine months old I miscarried a daughter. At this time, I was married
to the father of my second son, this baby and later another child. This was
my oldest son's stepfather.

After three children in three years my body said it needed a break, so
I miscarried. The doctor asked me if I wanted to know the sex of my baby
(after performing a D & C in his office with my boys sitting on the floor
playing). I told him "No".

He called a week later and said, "This is Dr. X and it's a girl"! I
immediately hung up. I vowed never to give him a single dime of the
money we owed him for my baby's birth, circumcision and the D & C. To

this day I never did. As a matter of fact, I filed bankruptcy on the balance I owed him. He probably even charged me for the time my baby was having seizures and we came into his office for assistance. He refused to help and gave me a tongue depressor to use. I knew not to place anything in my baby's mouth while they were seizing. It turns out karma is real as Dr. X died of cancer.

Thereafter, there is another child case that I become aware of. I asked my mom to watch my child while I went to court yet again and testify. She said, "Why can't you stay out of it? Keep your mouth shut!" Then she asked me why this was so important to me? I told her the only thing I could, "Because mom, it happened to me". My mom started crying and acting hysterical as if she hadn't known. My dad, hearing the noise, comes downstairs to ask what was going on and mom fills him in. This was the first my dad had ever heard of me being molested. They both ask for details and my dad leaves four hours early for work. We assume he is trying to find the two men who had molested me. We did not find out until he came home at midnight that he was unable to find them. Thank God! We were sure that if he had found the perpetrators, he would have killed them for sure.

My mom, in a fit about what had happened to me all those years ago, took me to a counselor in a large nearby city to help me heal even though we never talked about it. I believe that she should have known that something was amiss. The whole counseling experience was extremely negative. It was a bomb that was waiting to go off.

When we got there, my mom kept my baby out in the waiting room while I went in. The counselor proceeded to ask me questions. "Tell me what happened?" she asked. I told her the beginning of my story starting from about five years old on. I was only in the room for approximately 15 minutes. I honestly do not remember any of the specific questions. I only remember that we did not get very far before she looked down at my pregnant stomach and then looked past me towards the waiting room where my baby and mother were and said, "Don't you think you deserved it?" I was instantly furious! The voice inside me erupted...I said, "Excuse me? What child of five needs to act sexy for a man who is babysitting me? What child of five DESERVES this?" I walked out, picked up my son and told my mother, "If you pay her a dime, I will never speak to you again."

To this day I cannot tell you anything about her, except the perfume she wore was White Shoulders, she had an office in a nearby city, she was female and very wrong in her "assessment". If I had remembered any additional information, I would have gone back to end her business. Honestly, if she continued to counsel in that way, she probably would have lost her business long ago.

Throughout the early parts of my marriage, I hoped that my high school sweetheart would return and take us away on his white horse. I watch and wait, though it never happens. I was abused mentally, physically, emotionally and sexually, (including being raped) by my ex husband. Before long I am just a doormat for him. However, I see changes in my boys that I'm not comfortable with. Suddenly they are hitting me and yelling at me as well. When I said, "Don't do that", I would hear the boy's reply back, "Why not, daddy does it?" A voice then rears up in me saying, "My children will never be like their father."

A plan formed. All I needed was the date. I had a whole bottle of prescription painkillers that I had to use for constant migraines. I was going to give my boys a handful and take the rest of the bottle myself. In my mind I had the bottle divided into half for myself then the other half would be divided between my children. After all, I could not let them become like their father and we were unable to escape from his clutches. In many small ways I taught them it was ok to do the things their father and stepfather had done by my silence. After all, they saw it day in and day out.

If it were not for a program my children were enrolled in, that was always looking for ways to help us, we would not be here today. As I said earlier, I had a plan, just not the date of implementation. They did not know about all the abuse, but I am certain they suspected. They got us into counseling, parenting and domestic violence classes.

At this time, I am fed up with my husband's drinking, womanizing, cheating and abuse, as well as what it has done to our children. I joined a domestic violence group and they advised me how to leave the relationship. I knew that I had to leave or die! He had left me on the floor so many times bloody, broken and bruised for my children to find. This had to have been emotionally traumatizing for my children. If I died, then my boys would have been left with their dad and that was not an option. I could not, would not leave them to act like my ex-husband.

To go out shopping, I would wait until my drunk husband passed out. It was the only time I felt safe leaving the boys with him and they were all sleeping by then. I also thought shopping at midnight or two and three in the morning would be safe and I would not run into anyone I knew. Unfortunately, this ended up not being the case many times. The person I would see would always ask (when I did see people that I knew), if I was ok. I would always sadly reply with my eyes lowered, "Yes". Many times, it was the same person.

In one instance of abuse, my husband had come home from a night of drinking. I was at the sink doing dishes avoiding eye contact and he came at me swinging. I was running around the dining room table and eventually went under it to avoid him and came up again and there he was. He struck me so hard that when my temple hit the refrigerator the Admiral emblem was indented in the skin of my temple and cut my eyebrow. All I could see was red cascading like a waterfall into my eyes. It was like I had put on a pair of red glasses and everything was tinted red. I went back around the table and headed to the phone because I had had enough. I was going to call the police. I must have passed out as I was reaching for the phone, which was placed up high so the kids couldn't answer it. The next morning my kids had found me crumpled on the floor with a bloody handprint that smeared down the wall like mysterious graffiti where I had fallen trying to reach the phone. He then went to bed, as usual when these situations happened. He would usually ask me what happened the next day when he awoke. I so many times wanted to say, "Oh I did this to myself to make you think you had done it. "

Later, in my second marriage (approximately ten years later), I was hanging out with some people, having a ladies night. The combination of the three of our voices must have triggered my son because he came down the stairs with tears in his eyes having awoken from a dream, obviously distraught. He started describing a nightmare that he had just had. He starts telling us about the dream that he had in which he experienced this exact episode. We were floored that this meant that he had witnessed this whole horrific beating. We then informed him that this was not a dream and that they were present the morning after and had found me beaten and bloody on the floor.

After five years of my first marriage my high school sweetheart re-enters my life. We started talking, trying to clear up some of the misunderstandings from the past. He admitted that he was scared. His mom gave him an "out" by saying that I was sleeping around. So, he left and continued his life. He seemed to know just what to say to get this bruised, beaten and wounded ego back into a relationship with him.

I started looking for a house for the boys and I to live in because I was leaving my husband. I found a house and arranged to work on it in exchange for deposits. Often my current husband would help me with the house. He would help paint, clean out the house and make simple repairs, etc.

When it was time for us to move. I still had not told my husband that he was not going with us. I had gotten a restraining order against him as advised by the domestic violence group members. All his items were in his truck and mine and the boys items were in our vehicle or were already at the house.

On the way to the house with the last load, I had been rehearsing with the boys what to do. The kids dutifully ran into the house to hide as we discussed. I had copies of the restraining order and the lease (without his name on it) right by the door. I picked it and the phone up and dialed 911. I raised up his copy of the restraining order and lease and stated that he had better leave as I was calling 911. I told the 911 operator my location and that I had a restraining order and that my husband was on the premises and his presence was unwanted.

Instantly he was his usual abusive self. He started screaming that he would kill me and that he was going to come back and take my babies. Then, he heard sirens and sped off. It was not over, not by a long shot. He would drive by, screaming obscenities and threats out of his truck. We now had a chance to learn a new life without abuse.

One of my brother-in-law's told me that it was not fair to say that I am a domestic violence survivor. As if I am supposed to shrink my truth to make others more comfortable and my story more palatable? Nope, not my problem! Besides, I have plenty of witnesses to prove my case.

For months, the kids had nightmares about him coming to steal them. They would not sleep in their own rooms for more than six months. There was also a lot of reprogramming I had to do. My middle child had dropped a milk carton when headed back to the breakfast table one morning. Immediately melting into tears apologizing because a mess had been made. I knelt in the milk, in my pajamas (with my baby) and assured them all that this was "Ok", that we would simply clean it up. That was all. It broke my heart that they felt so bad about small mistakes. Dropping things, leaving toys out, talking excitedly or just simply being kids. It took a long time to correct the past, but I gave it everything I had. I had to. They were and still are so important to me. They were, still are and always will be my life.

Also, during this time, I babysat to make money. I worked for one lady who was a horrible mother, she had four or five kids and was a drug/alcohol addict. Her youngest child lived with us often. The older children were too young to take care of the baby. The children lived in her car while she was in the bars. This happened because she could not find anyone to watch them. She and the father who was in jail, eventually gave me permission to adopt the baby.

About four days before we were scheduled to go to court for the adoption of the child, the maternal grandparents came with the police and took her from my high school sweetheart, my boys and me.

The local police did not even read the note that I had received from the mother and father with explicit and specific instructions stating that she did not want her alcoholic parents getting her children. Because I was not a biological family member, the police did not seem to care that we never saw the baby again.

The boys and I were heartbroken and devastated. We did finally see her later and it broke all our hearts. She looked like a little ragamuffin girl, clothes too large and hair disheveled. But I did all I could have done for her. At least she knew she was loved for that small amount of time we had her.

I often babysat for others, but often got excuses why I could not be paid. I had to tell them I could not watch their children anymore. My welfare check was short for the rent and I had to make it up somewhere. The only way that I could make up the difference was by babysitting.

Sadly, this experience taught me many things, many that I wish I did not know, but sadly cannot un-know. However, I learned much that has served me well. Such as, I can stretch out a budget by saving leftover veggies that were uneaten, placing them in an empty ice cream bucket and freezing it. At the end of the month I would make a stew.

I can make a meal out of three ingredients: a can of cream of mushroom soup, noodles and a can of pork or chicken from the government. It makes what I called "pig surprise" and my children as well as many others loved it. Now we add mushrooms and parmesan cheese, but to me this meal reminds me of a time when there was little or no food in the house and of the struggles I had to face during that time.

---

Deuteronomy 4:9 - "Only take heed to thyself, and keep thy soul diligently, lest thou forget the things which thine eyes have seen, and lest they depart from thy heart all the days of thy life: but teach them thy sons, and thy sons' sons."

---

# 4

*Changing the Fate of My Future*

*"A small behavioral change can also lead to embracing
a wider checklist of healthier choices."*

CHUCK NORRIS

S ADLY, MY PARENTS WERE NOT good parents. So, I decided to take
every opportunity to change how I was going to parent. My children
were enrolled in an early childhood education program when they were
four and they offered parenting classes. I took these classes every time they
were offered. Every time I learned something new and I began to get much
stronger and more confident in my role as a parent. I learned so much! It
turns out I took the classes four years in a row! I ended up taking the class
seven times overall. The boys having birthdays later in the year allowed
us another year in the program! I was a little sponge soaking up the rays
of the sun to my soul.

I could have chosen to stay in ignorance of my learned bad behaviors.
I could have chosen to be like my parents, but I did not like how I had
been treated, so I knew I had to change.

I was not perfect as a parent. I slipped back into the way my parents
had chosen to parent more times than I can count and then I would be
mortified by my actions. I would pick up my Exploring Parenting manual
again and again and trudge on knowing that I had to do better than my

parents had done for me. This is something I had wished was done by my parents as well. But they did not, and I could and did! Things were different for me and my children!

I was so proud of who we were becoming. I was seeing my children blossom, grow and thrive under what I had learned. It was an amazing feeling. Changing the fate of our future is powerful!

I learned healthy boundaries, how to choose corrective discipline, how to use firm but loving words and rules and I learned about respect-vs-fear. I desired for my children to respect me, not because they feared me. I also wanted them to be different then their stepfather and father and not abuse women. I wanted their lives to be better and much different than mine was as a child. I feared my father, and out of that fear I respected him. I wanted my children to respect and not fear me.

It was not easy! As a matter of fact, it was incredibly challenging. To change a tape that had been running in your head for all these years. To choose to put in a new one while facing giants in your mind and risking disapproval from your parents and siblings.

Many times, I was told by a few family members that I was making a mistake by giving my children the option to say how they feel. I have never regretted it! Stating your opinion is not talking back if it is done with respect and honesty. My children were taught that they too have a voice and they can say how they feel.

As a child I can remember many times when my father would express his opinion about something or make a comment in general. When I disagreed with him it usually went like this: if you have an opinion that is not like mine, you do not have an opinion. I was not allowed to say how I felt. If I did not agree with his opinion, then my opinion was not valid. So many times, when I was younger and even as I grew older, I would think inside my head that I did not agree with him on a certain subject, but I kept it to myself to keep the peace. With my children I wanted them to feel that their opinions were valid and important. That they could express their opinions and that I could answer questions and we could converse freely even if we disagreed.

I wanted so much more for my children then I had as a child. As a result of this desire, we conversed at dinner time, had weekly family meetings and voted on family decisions. We were all given equal rights in our home, even though as mom I could overrule decisions as needed. I carefully weighed and explained my decisions as though they were smart enough to understand (I believe they were) and then we would talk about the decisions and plan accordingly. This allowed them to realize that they were important and that their input was valued. They then had the ability to see things that were outside of their realm. I believe that it helped them grow as well. This was especially helpful to them in so many ways as growing young men.

They were starting to see that they had roles in our family. However, I did one thing very differently from many other parents I have known. I decided that each of my children were responsible for themselves, and that the oldest was never responsible for the younger siblings. I believed that my oldest was and should never be held responsible for the younger children. When they were old enough to leave home, they would be accountable for their own behaviors. I did not allow them to tattle on each other, call each other names or treat each other with disrespect. These behaviors were highly frowned upon and correctly dealt with in our home.

I wanted a home that was kind, loving and safe. This was something I never felt in my childhood home, the home I shared with my first husband, and then later with my high school sweetheart/boyfriend.

I also changed many other things from my childhood. This included abuse, neglect, and isolation (ignoring) us kids. We were not separated from the bad behavior that we had performed. Therefore we felt like we were bad kids.

One thing I learned from the parenting class is that you need to separate the child from their bad behavior. If you do not, then the child believes that they are bad themselves. I chose to use positive words with my children; not screaming, yelling, cursing and saying terrible things to them or hitting them for no apparent reason.

It was hard but so rewarding to see my children have a childhood. My children were correctly disciplined, shown love, reason and understanding. I learned how to use age appropriate tactics to correct behaviors, teach and instill pride and self-esteem.

It was an amazing feeling to grasp these new ways and see the impact they were having on my children. It was impacting their future and I knew that this would also affect the future of my grandchildren someday in a positive way.

Yes! Yes, I say! I did it! I am SO PROUD of what I did!

---

Ecclesiastes 8:1 - "Who is as the wise man? And who knoweth the interpretation of a thing? A man's wisdom maketh his face to shine, and the boldness of his face shall be changed."

---

# 5

## False Hope

*"And as far as false hope, there is no such thing. There is only hope or the absence of hope-nothing else."*

PATTI DAVIS

AFTER THINGS SETTLED DOWN, AS much as they could, my boyfriend encouraged me to start working on the divorce. This was ridiculously hard, because I had believed that marriage was forever, and that I had failed. However, I quickly learned that I could only take half the blame. You cannot make a relationship work if you are the only one trying!

Finally, court day rolled around, and I was scared and ecstatic. I could marry my boyfriend now! When I arrived at court, I was so nervous that my soon to be ex-husband would show up but he did not. The judge kept asking me if there was anything I wanted? I kept saying, "My children, my car and my freedom." He asked me three or four times, and my answer was the same. He said, "You can have whatever you want, as he isn't here to defend himself." Even after explaining to the judge that my ex would never do anything he said, I still said, "My children, my car and my freedom." Finally, he hit the gavel against the sound block and said, "Granted". The gavel landed so hard that it scared me, I jumped and thought I was going to wet myself. I did not. But I did skip out of that courtroom and I am quite sure the judge thought I was off my rocker. I was relieved that I had protected my children, secured their safety and now we had a chance to start again.

After this time period, my boyfriend moved in with us. I thought we could finally be a family without abuse. I learned that abuse takes on many different forms. Just because he did not hit me, this does not mean that there was no abuse. I assumed he loved me because he would hold my hand and kiss me in public. My ex-husband would not show any public displays of affection because he thought I was too fat. He used to say I was fat, ugly and no one was ever going to love me.

My boyfriend and I often fought. There was mistrust on his part and accusations of cheating. I could never come close to the magnitude of how he had hurt me. He would call me terrible names. Again, seeing the same tattle tale signs, my children began treating me the way both their dad and stepdad had. I told him he could take back all the nasty things he had said about me or we were leaving. He chose not to, and we left that same day. I told my "little men" to pack up their bags that we were leaving. I could not see what my friends had been telling me about him and the way he had been treating me all along! I was oblivious.

Before I left he would listen to all my calls and then say I was making plans and that we were talking in code. It was ridiculous! All this time, he would take girls out to lunch at work. He would play footsie with them and that was ok, but If I bent over to pick something up off the floor and a man was there, I was "showing myself off". The jealousy was incredible and completely without measure.

"The clan" moved into the basement of my mother and dad's house in which the upper half was rented. We still saw my ex boyfriend off and on for a time wherein I was truly hoping that it would work out. But sadly, it never did. I had enough of being accused of cheating, being spoken to as though I were a second-class citizen and cleaning up the constant messes of him throwing plates of food that he did not like. I did not want my children to think that this behavior was acceptable for them to witness in their future.

We were not at my parent's home long when we were kicked out in the middle of winter having been accused of doing something I would never do. I later learned that the tenant had slept with my ex-husband and several other ex-boyfriends and thought I was retaliating by sleeping with her husband. I would never get even in any way from other people's actions or implications. I simply am not like that.

We were now homeless in the dead of winter. My mom and dad purchased an eighteen-foot travel trailer and moved it into a park in a local city. We were there for a month and a half and then moved to a larger nearby city. Once in a nearby campground, we were without power for a few days then we proceeded to move again to a park where we stayed for nine months. This place was a nice little park off of a local highway. We made a few friends, however, three rambunctious boys in a trailer was very taxing on all of us. There was always fighting and lack of room and NO personal space.

We ran out of food stamps often because it cost more to purchase smaller amounts than larger ones. When I was able to purchase larger amounts, there was not enough room to keep it in the small trailer. I only had small cabinets for food and dishes. I couldn't win!

We went to spend time "camping" with friends whenever we could. We spent nine months in the trailer although it felt more like a year.

Many things happened while we were there at this trailer park. Still angry with my family from the "retaliation incident", we did not go to the family Thanksgiving dinner. We were not having a particularly good start to the holiday season and Christmas did not look any more promising. A family member brought gifts and stockings for the boys. It was a Christmas miracle. I am still grateful because without it, there would not have been a Christmas that year!

During this time in the trailer, I had gone deaf in my right ear. I did not figure this out until one winter day when a friend called and I realized that I could not hear her. I held the receiver up to my right ear and I could not hear a thing. I assumed this was due to the trailer being so cold and that this ear was the one that was exposed to the cold the most. Little did I know that this hearing loss would hugely affect me later in life.

Thereafter, I ran into a friend I had known from an agency that our children had both attended. We struck up a conversation, we were both single and I felt like we might have a chance at a relationship.

At this time, I found out that we had finally received our housing! It was a long process. We looked at so many places and finally chose a third-floor apartment in a local suburb. It was not far from the current trailer park where we resided, so the boys did not have to change schools.

We were scheduled to move into our new apartment in January! The friend from the agency asked if he could help! I said, "Sure, that would be great!" We planned a party to celebrate after we were moved in. After we had been moving all day, it became late. I asked him to stay over. I stated that I was not ready to move forward with a physical relationship and he understood and agreed.

We both wanted to take things slowly and to do things right to make sure we had something worth building upon. Later that night, after the boys were asleep, a few friends came over and we had a few drinks. After everyone left, we went to bed together (sleeping). Later, there was a drastic change in the relationship and boundaries had been severely crossed.

I awoke to find him having sex with me. I said, "Hey we agreed not to do this!" and he said, "I'm almost finished." After he was "finished", I rolled myself over and cried myself to sleep. Once again, my trust in men had been shattered. I considered this rape as I had stated clearly that I did not want to start a physical relationship, and this was started without my permission. He left that next morning and we have never spoken since.

**"Nearly 1 in 5 women (18.3%) and 1 in 71 men (1.4%) in the United States have been raped at some time in their lives..."("Statistics", SVRC 2010 Summary Report, Sexual Violence by any Perpetrator, nsvrc.org)**

Since having my trust shattered so many times, I decided to play a little hard ball. I became the aggressor. I accepted a couple of men's monies for sex. I became a prostitute. I figured I needed money to raise my boys, and was not ready to trust again. Being a full-figured woman, it was not easy, there were still a few men who preferred larger women. It was not an exceptionally long or prosperous situation, and it basically backfired on me. I ended up going to the doctor, only to be told, "You have herpes, you will live, and hey, at least it's not AIDS." How comforting that doctor was. His bedside manner left something to be desired, for sure. Unfortunately, someone had herpes and did not share this little tidbit of information with me when we were intimate! No big surprise, I was once again devastated. My trust was broken, and I was once again thinking I was damaged merchandise, and that no one would ever want me.

My best friend at the time said I should not tell anyone I became involved with that I had herpes. We fought about this subject many times and finally I said "I will not be untruthful like the person who gave it to me."

When I felt I was ready to date again I placed an ad in the Thrifty Nickel newspaper date section. My first ad was not a success. I encountered many men who still lived with their mother, who were psycho's, had bad hygiene, etc. My boys were cleaner than some of the men that I ended up dating. I usually ended up dating the person only one time. My adopted brother was my hero! He would run off the unwanted affections of some of the men "a.k.a. "adult children".

However, my second ad was a much better match. I was a bit more specific about what I had wanted and did not want in a man. I did not want a momma's boy. I did not want a smoker and a heavy drinker. I explained that I was a plus sized woman, single mom, college student and that I had certain parameters. I met many new friends, and if I felt like we were going to be more than friends, I confided in them about the herpes. I was honest, a few were scared off and I respected that! At least I would not have guilt about my lack of honesty. After all, dishonesty is no way to start a new relationship.

After many dates I finally found one that I had a connection with. He was not afraid of herpes, my three boys or me. This was pretty much a miracle! The thing is I was at least an hour late for our first date. My aunt, cousin and her husband were visiting and I was trying not to be rude about it, but was trying to get dressed for my date. Eventually I just told them that I was sorry but I had a date that night. I was so scared when we finally arrived that he wouldn't be there. But he and his friends were and we had a great time talking, playing pool and darts. We started calling each other regularly and he was so easy to talk to. Although initially I was more attracted to his friend, I came to rely on his stability, kindness and genuine care for me and my children. I was slow to react and respond out of fear of my past relationships, but his patience was rewarded.

Job 8:13 - "So are the paths of all that forget God; and the hypocrite's hope shall perish."

# 6

Stepmom and Stepdad

*"When any of us thinks of ourselves as a role model - whether
that's as a parent being observed by their kids or a leader under
the microscope of their followers - it creates a natural stepping up
of how we carry ourselves and what we expect from ourselves."*

CHIP CONLEY

T HIS NEW MAN'S NAME WAS George. George and I started dating and
we introduced our children to one another. We started doing things
together as a family.

Blending two families was extremely hard! Although, I always said
that I would never date a guy who had kids as I had enough of my own.
But often what we say and do are two entirely different things! Honestly
five kids in a household was nightmarish, harried and wonderful too. The
kids often had friends over and I learned to cook for an army. As a matter
of fact, I still cook for an army even after all the children have come and
gone again and again! Life was a roller coaster ride. We struggled so much
to have a healthy happy home! The one thing I think we did exceptionally
well was treat ALL the children like they were ours! Not MINE or YOURS,
but OURS. The only "ours" we have ever had was the furbabies.

We went through hades and back for our children. When I first met
George's girls, I felt like I had just taken Tarzan out of the jungle! They

had not gone anywhere, they were lacking in social skills and they did not know how to act in public, let alone at home. I had to teach them about bathing and how to wear clothing such as dresses and behave like civilized humans.

After George and I had decided to become a family. I decided to make a "pact" to do what was best for all the children, with or without the other parents' participation. As part of this pact I went to his ex wife's house to see if she was game for treating each other with respect and doing what was best for the girls. George offered to go with me and I said, "No, this is between her and I." I went while the girls were at school so they would not be present while our interaction happened. I knocked on her door and she opened it, I said, " I am aware that you don't like me, and honestly the feeling is mutual. But for the sake of our girls, I would like to make a pact with you where we honor each other, at least in front of the girls." She looked me up and down and said some choice words and slammed the door in my face. I still honored the other parents' position in their life even when I secretly hated them. Though I no longer hate them, I sure pity them. After all they were missing out on some amazing kids.

I was called mom and George was called dad even though we were not biologically related. We were the reason our family thrived. We were the reason they did well. We were a blended family.

I believe that if my daughter had lived, I would have closed my heart to any future daughters. I believe I had miscarried for two reasons: 1) my heart would have been full as my longing for a daughter would have already been full and 2) I never would have been able to give that love to any other girls because I would have had what my heart wanted and sought. I was so needed. Boy was I ever.

It was rough, but I knew that the Lord wanted me to do this! Though there were times when I shouted at Him, "Lord I didn't break them, why do I have to fix them?" But, looking back and seeing how horribly the girls were treated by their mother, I am so glad I did. I know beyond a shadow of a doubt that their abuse would have continued, and that one if not both-of-them would have committed suicide like their stepbrother did later in life.

When we found out that the stepbrother had committed suicide, the girls were in their early teens. I went with them to the funeral knowing I was stepping into unsafe waters. This was their mother's territory. I was their mom, and I could never let my children go to a family funeral alone. They needed me! I needed them and I was on their side. There were a select few people who were on my side. They checked on me regularly by giving me occasional eye contact and mouthing, "Are you ok?" during the funeral and reception.

At one time the girl's mother walked up to me, threw her arms around me and tearfully thanked me for loving her daughters as much as she loved her step son. The girls were both very alarmed by her behavior, as was I. I never once believed for a minute that this was truly authentic. It was just a ploy. The girls had told me that she beat that step son into a corner and one of the girls had to stop her. This happened just a week before they had found him hanging not even 12 feet or so away from their home when he committed suicide.

**"You were born with the ability to change someone's life. Don't ever waste it." (author unknown, www. livelifehappy.com).**

---

Colossians 3:20 - "Children, obey your parents in all things: for this is well pleasing unto the Lord."

---

# 7

*His Plan Not Mine*

*"What I've learned is that unless it's an emergency, like a fire or brain surgery, hierarchy is not necessary and may be damaging. If you have a hierarchy, you're repeating the strengths and weaknesses of one person without allowing for the accumulative strength of a group."*

GLORIA STEINEM

"IMAGINE IF YOU WILL, BEING on your deathbed. And standing around your bed are the ghosts of the ideas, the dreams, the abilities, the talents given to you by life.

And that you-for whatever reason-you never acted on those ideas, you never pursued that, you never used those talents, we never saw your leadership, you never used your voice, you never wrote your book.

And there they are, standing around your bed looking at you with large, angry eyes, saying, "We came to you, and only you could have given us life! Now we must die with you forever.

The question is: If you died today, what ideas, what dreams, what abilities, what talents, what gifts would die with you?"

*Unstoppable Influence. Be You. Be Fearless. Transform Lives.* Natasha Hazlett

One day I ended up going to the emergency room with a screaming earache. I wanted to scream because it hurt so bad. I asked the physician, "How can I have an ear infection in an ear that I can't hear out of?" He said: "(1) those are not related, (2) you can still hear in an ear that has an infection." I finally was able to understand what my middle son had been experiencing most of his childhood. This ER visit triggered MRI's, CAT scans and hearing tests. These test results indicated the diagnosis of a tumor. I was about to embark on a huge journey.

I was diagnosed with a non-cancerous brain tumor. An acoustic neuroma. It was located behind my right ear between the ear and the brain stem under the temporal lobe of the brain. I had to have brain surgery as soon as possible. The surgery date did not seem soon enough to me as surgery was scheduled for a few months after that!

Brain surgery was a nightmare experience. If I would have been able to talk about it without going into hysteria, I might own the entire hospital the procedure was performed at right now. The first night after the surgery I was the primary patient in the ICU, right off the nurse's station. They closed my window and door and had a party in the nurse's station. They were supposed to turn me every thirty minutes. I had a large steel needle in my spinal cord to drain excess fluid. Therefore, it was important to keep my body moving. My legs would go numb if I were not turned regularly. In order to be consistently turned I had to use the call light. They would ignore it.

For seven days and nights this was what happened. I was extremely nauseated and I could not eat. I stayed awake all night to make sure that they were doing their job. So, I was sleeping all day and therefore missed all my visitors. I thought no one had come to see me. I was so depressed and I thought no one loved me. I thought that I was just left there alone for seven days.

They infiltrated my IV, and my arm swelled up to the size of my leg. They ran out of pressure wound material and used gauze and tied it in knots. This caused scarring and horrible headaches. The scars on my forehead are constant reminders that I overcame this ordeal.

One day I awoke to see my mom slipping out of the door, I cried out for her, "Mom don't leave me here!" She heard my cry. As best as I could, I explained through tears and sobbing from the trauma I had been through and for once in my life my mother stood up for me.

**"Out of suffering have emerged the strongest souls; the most massive characters are seared with scars." Kahill Gibran**

It was horrible, but the worst thing I endured while in ICU was not being able to see my boys! I had seven days without being able to see them. I sunk into a deep, deep depression. How could they not allow visitors under the age of 18? I was not allowed visitors and was receiving awful care. Most importantly, I was not allowed to see my boys. They would not let anyone open the window to my room. It was horrible. When I was finally moved out of the ICU to the regular floor, the care was awesome.

I will never forget the night the boys came to see me. I could hear their cowboy boots clomping down the hall to my room. I was so excited! They were, still are, and always will be my world. George said the minute they found out they could see me, they all ran for the shower, dressed in their best, combed their hair and brushed their teeth! They did not stay long as I was still very tired. I had to turn my sleeping pattern around from staying awake all night to keep the nurses on their job.

After they left, that night, I found I could not sleep. I tried and tried, but It was a no go. There is a church that is close to the hospital. They have a huge cross that lights up. I felt like the cross was taunting me and I was mad that I had lived because I had planned to die. I asked the nurses to close the curtain, and it shined through anyway. I then asked them to close the inner curtains, but it also shone through them. I put the blankets over my head, and it shined through that! You know what they say about when you are down and out, "Look up"! Finally, in exhaustion I said, "God what do you want?" I did not hear an audible voice, it was in my spirit and He showed me plain as day, a vision. He showed me the battle that occurred during my brain surgery. Satan was trying to take me under. As much as that is what I truly wanted at that moment GOD knew there was so much more for me to do here. This happened when I quit breathing after an eighteen and one-half hour surgery. But I am still here!

They placed breathing tubes in my nose and mouth and a mask on my face. I survived and came up off the table. That was a battle and God won. During the vision I asked Him, "Why me and what have I ever done to deserve this ?" In my head I saw images of my boys, my three precious boys. There were visions of Jesus going to hell and stealing the keys of the kingdom back from satan. This was when I went through brain surgery and Jesus was fighting satan to keep me alive. It says in Matthew 16:19, "I will give you the keys to the kingdom of heaven; whatever you bind on earth will be bound in heaven and whatever you loose on earth will be loosed in heaven." (NIV)

The audible voice said that I had always done right by my boys, that my work here was not done and that Jesus would have gone to hell to get those keys even if it were only for me. I broke, I broke that wall, the dam that I had built so high and tight around my heart. I cried, which I had never really done much of. I cried at a snowflake, a leaf that fell, at pretty much everything! But it was happy tears now.

The tumor killed my balance, hearing and severely damaged my facial nerve. My face does not work as it had before. My eye does not cry (which makes me angry) and my balance is only controlled by one side of my body. My vision helps to keep my balance so going places in the dark is very treacherous. I am completely deaf in my right ear and am missing several decibels in my left ear (probably just like my dad had said when he yelled to turn that music down all those years).

I now wear hearing aids in both ears. The one in my right ear is a transmitter sending sounds to my left ear, which makes it difficult for me to know which side noise is coming from, but I can hear! But even through all these difficulties I know I would have missed so much! Oh, thank God that He has a plan.

I had to learn how to eat and drink as the facial muscles were damaged from the surgery. It was embarrassing and it made me angry and hostile. One time I pushed George's hand away as he was lovingly wiping food or slobber off my chin that I did not know was there. I was angry that I had lived. I was planning on passing away during the surgery. The boys were old enough to make it, they had plenty of people in their lives. They were old enough to remember me. Thankfully that didn't happen. The things I wouldn't have witnessed!

There were many challenges then, but these challenges paled in comparison to what I have been able to enjoy in my life since. The struggles have built character and made me who I am. Oh, but what I would have missed...oh my goodness. It took quite a while, about four years, for me to be happy about living. I just think about what I would have missed, and it sure changes my attitude.

---

Hebrews 13:21 - "Make you perfect in every good work to do his will, working in you that which is well pleasing in his sight, through Jesus Christ."

---

# 8

—※—

## *Angel*

*"You might be temporary in their life, they might be temporary in yours, but there is nothing temporary about the love or the lesson."*

TONYA CHRISTLE

WHEN I FIRST SAW THE kid, they slinked in late and always left early from the church we attended. I couldn't figure out if they were a girl or a boy. God began to nudge me to talk to them and of course I said, "Lord I have enough with five kids". As always, when He wants me to do something, He keeps at it, bugging me until I give in. One day I left our pew, and moved to the end of the one they were in. I kept scooting closer, trying to make eye contact. I cannot even remember how and when it happened, but I learned she was a girl and her name was Angel.

We started our friendship. I felt responsible for her. She became like one of our kids, or my little niece. She came for dinner once a week and then we would go to church. We added her to our family and did things with her. She grew, learned and loved us, and we loved her.

A time came when the church we were attending was not a safe nor a Godly place. George, our family and I left the church. A niggling in my mind would not go away. It was a thought that they would use and hurt Angel that would not go away. I called her and explained this to her in detail. She started attending our church. She remained at this church until her death.

Sadly, we had a rift and even more sadly it was never mended before her death. When I attended her funeral, my heart was so broken because of this rift. Since we were unable to mend the disagreement we missed so much of each other's lives.

Yearly Angel would go down to the Fort for the Fourth of July. This time she wanted us to pick her up. The Fort was a 19th century trading post that was the headquarters for the Hudson's Bay Trading Company. This is a historic monument and it had the best fireworks in the area.

Because it was so late, she offered to pay us for the ride. We did not want to take her money, but she was insistent because of the inconvenience. After making a promise based upon that money Angel was going to give us, she changed her mind and asked someone else to pick her up. It made me mad because I hate it when someone breaks promises. I should have been more graceful and forgiving.

With that being said, I was also in a place of growth and transition. I did try to talk to her several times, and we were never able to get past it. I loved her and loved seeing the world through her eyes! I miss her. The other day I saw a young woman riding her bike and had to remember it was not her.

Angel was exuberant, funny and silly. She was loving and very caring, loud, funny and thoughtful. Angel loved to take pictures and then scrapbook them. She usually went everywhere with us, sometimes to the chagrin of my boys. She had no impulse control so there was much teaching, learning and growing. We talked about how others would feel if they were being belittled, being called silly names, or how they may feel embarrassed.

I was so proud of Angel as she always kept a clean and tidy home, cooked and baked for others and kept herself clean and neat as well. It was so beautiful to watch her emerge as a beautiful young woman.

As you remember when I first met her, I had no idea that she was a young girl. She started caring about her hair and clothes. She started getting haircuts regularly and choosing different styles that she found appealing and flattering. She would wear barrettes and pony-tails and let her hair grow out also. It was a beautiful transformation watching her become a beautiful young woman of God.

As she studied the Bible she changed and grew. I loved when she would grab onto something you said and you could see it in her eyes. She would then use it in her everyday life. We would have many conversations about what certain scriptures meant and how to apply them.

Angel was very smart, but often missed how things worked together and needed an explanation in a way she could understand. We spent many evenings, phone calls and weekly dinners developing her understanding. What a blessing and a labor of love our relationship was, and I miss her still to this day.

Angel was also responsible for helping us find our daughters when their mother ran with them and was hiding them from us for three years. What a blessing Angel was in our lives.

---

Luke 20:36 - "Neither can they die any more: for they are equal unto the angels; and are the children of God, being the children of the resurrection."

---

# 9

### ❦

## *Speaking Ill*

*"Don't paint a nasty picture of your exes. We'll justifiably wonder what made you stay in those heinous situations in the first place."*

LIZ VASSEY

I OFTEN SOUGHT THE ADVICE OF a very dear friend. With her guidance I believe I was/am an exemplary ex-wife. She always advised me to never speak ill of a child's parents in their presence. This served me so superbly in the case of my children as well as with my ex-husband and many other close relationships. It was so hard, but this was the best thing I ever did for our family. I generally only talked about the ex's to George, my counselor or my friends.

Mental, verbal, emotional, physical, sexual abuse and rape are never ok. I was victimized by my ex-husband and many others as well. I can say that when It comes to marriage I had no idea what *for better or worse* really meant. His version and my version really were two different things We often held very different values. Their version of cheating was totally different than mine. It was ok for them but not you. Do as I say, not as I do so to speak. This included cheating, lying, having secret conversations with the opposite sex, breaking trust, risking our financial security by racking up several credit cards for adult sites, drinking, smoking away their paychecks, or a myriad of other things.

I was caring for our children when I did not speak ill of their parents.

A lot of people do not understand that when you speak ill of a child's parents, you are in essence speaking ill of the child themselves (because they are a part of them).

As an early childhood educator, I have a lot of knowledge about children and self-esteem, as well as emotional health and wellness. Under that umbrella I worked hard to ensure that all our children were protected, as well as feeling safe in our home. A lot of people do not understand that we are our children's first educators. As shown in the story below, I am constantly trying to be a positive role model to our children.

One day an unwanted person showed up in our yard and was verbally abusive, throwing and breaking things and threatening our family. At this time, we had a one hundred and twenty-five pound, rottweiler, chow and shepherd mix. He was reacting very negatively to this intruder. All five children were encouraging me to let the dog go and take care of the problem. I did not feel that this was an appropriate thing for the children to see and encouraged the intruder to leave the property. Eventually the intruder left the premises and we were all allowed to talk about the situation. The younger children all felt threatened and scared. The older ones were more amused by watching the dog go ballistic. I was neither amused nor happy about the situation but chose to take the "higher ground" and do what was best for all parties included. The saddest part of this was that that intruder was the girl's mothers boyfriend. He was given our address from their mother. The simple fact that she allowed him to drive here drunk and threaten our household with her children present really bothered me. But again, I chose the high road.

I would like to believe that the choices that I have made were the best for all our children. Every decision that I made was wrought with their safety, concern, wellness and wholeness in mind.

Whatever the other people feel they did, did not, could, should and would have done is between themselves and God. He knows the truth regarding these relationships. All we can do is do our best. We are only responsible for our part in our relationships and I feel like I did just that! I will just leave that there.

Psalms 34:13 - "Keep thy tongue from evil, and thy lips from speaking guile."

# 10

## Healing vs. Anguish

*"It took me a while to learn the true meaning of patience and surrender, but I have finally accepted that healing doesn't happen on our schedule. It doesn't have a clock or a calendar."*

YOLANDA HADID

WE HAD GONE THROUGH SOME horrible church situations and finally moved on to a church body that we were happy with. At this church there was so much change and growth. I found a counselor who helped me more than she will ever know, and I am eternally grateful she showed me how to live and not just merely survive, but to thrive!

The kids and George were not quite sure what to expect when I came home from counseling. In the past, counseling would make me angry and stirred up way more than I could ever deal with. Usually I would come home as angry as a bucket full of pit vipers that someone has stirred up with a stick, ready to bite anyone and everyone in my sight. But this time it was way different. I was happy, finally growing and healing over some of the junk that I had gone through.

I was able to forgive my abusers and many others. I am still in the process of forgiving. It is not easy! But it is worth it. I remember working on forgiving my molesters and telling my counselor I did not think I ever could.

We went to Walmart one night and George and the kids ran in, I had a headache and was waiting out in the van with the engine running so we could get home quickly. This was a big, eighteen passenger Ford Econoline van. I then see this guy walking head down, almost walking into the nose of the van. He had to have heard it idling or saw the headlights blaring. Then he raised his head at the right front side of the van and our eyes locked, I could not look away nor did I feel he could either. I was thinking, "Oh no, my doors are not locked." I instantly recognized him as one of my molesters, the one who hurt me the most. My hand dropped to the gear shift, my foot went to the brake pedal and I revved the engine. As he moved across the front of the van to the driver's door, I saw misery, pain, suffering and anguish in his eyes. Not at all what I was expecting.

Now standing at the driver's side door of the van, a few feet away, our eyes were still magnetically locked on one another. It felt like static electricity. As quickly as it started, the connection ended, just broke, and he lowered his head, turned away and went to his car leaving me extremely shaken.

Funny thing is, I thought the people who hurt me all just skipped away and lived life happily ever after, after ruining my childhood and probably many others as well. What I had believed all this time was not true and it was such an eye opener. Then a week or so later I saw him at a burger joint with his son and again there was no joy, fun, or enjoying the time he had with his child. Again seeing him and his son at the same burger joint and the same thing. No joy, happiness, no buoyant conversations. This time, a new emotion came over me, pity and maybe some sorrow.

Talking with my counselor was hard, but we were starting to see some forgiveness come around. I can now say I forgave the men who molested me. I would have liked to tell them that there is a Savior that can help. I tried to find them, to send them a letter but I was unsuccessful.

Now that I am processing it, the abuse was abuse whether they labeled me their girlfriend or not. The anger was directed at the two who were at the beginning of the abuse. They physically and sexually hurt me. The others did not, but it was still sexual abuse and It was inappropriate!

weirdly enough I had heard that both of the men had died. Imagine walking around in Walmart and running into someone who you thought was dead. Yes, it happened!

I was just leaving an aisle and turning right and looked up and there he was, right in front of me turning towards me from the aisle he was on. My mind was splitting. Here I was seeing him, and my mind and my body were arguing. One was saying, "He's dead", the other was saying, "He's right here. Wait a minute…you cannot dismiss the truth. It was right in front of me." I simply turned and shakily went to find George.

Later that evening, through Facebook Messenger, I reached out to his ex-wife. We were friends from school and I asked her if he had passed on. She said no, he was alive and living nearby. Wow! Someone had told me that he had passed away. It was from a local high school Facebook site that I had learned this information.

In Lysa Terkeursts book, *Forgiving What You Can't Forget,* makes this statement and it's one I think every person who has been victimized should hear. "Whether this was an event or a collection of hurt that built over time because someone wasn't who they were supposed to be, didn't do what they were supposed to do, or didn't protect you like they should have protected you, your heartbreak deserves a safe place to be processed. Whoever 'they' are in your story, their actions hurt you, took from you, and set off a chain of events still greatly affecting you. And that was wrong. Your pain is real. And so is mine. So if no one has acknowledged this with you, I will."

Wow, how did that make you feel? For me it was MONUMENTAL! to be heard, felt, seen and acknowledged for what I have been through. It makes all the difference, takes a weight off your shoulders and sets you free. It's like someone unlocked the gate that had held us captive with our truth. Oh my goodness. What a relief it is to stop carrying that burden.

If you are in a relationship where it hurts, or if you have a feeling that it is wrong, it probably is! Your conscience is that little voice inside, and I would trust it if I were you! It may not be easy to listen to, you may not want to leave that relationship, but you are worth having good happen to you! Did you hear that? <u>You are worth having good happen to you!</u> Sometimes you must choose to let good happen to you! Let people love you, and care for you. Let people in! Yes, I know they can hurt you! Oh, how well I know. If you do not let people in then you are just getting by. I would rather be hurt then not feel at all. Feeling is living.

Remember earlier in the book when I talked about being inside my cave, dark, cold, and lonely? That is not living, that is merely surviving.

Also, during this time, I had a huge realization. I was cautious of the fact that I was molested because the statistics (I also researched a lot of stuff to become knowledgeable) stated that **"23% of the perpetrators (people who commit sexual abuse) had experienced sexual abuse with physical contact in childhood. "** ("Sexual Abuse in the Childhood of Perpentrators", Karine Baril, Institut national de sante publique du Quebec (INSPQ) mobile, inspq.qc.ca).

> **"About one in seven girls and one in twenty-five boys will be sexually abused before they turn 18. (Darkness to Light, "Child Sexual Abuse Statistics", d2l.org).**

That was so frightening to me! So, I was incredibly careful with the boys. I would not allow them to sleep in our bed. I taught them very early how to wash all their body parts, I wouldn't snuggle or overly cuddle them. Anything I could do to minimize an opportunity to hurt them as I had been hurt. All this time it never dawned on me that I wasn't like that! I never had thoughts or desires to hurt them. Praise God I broke yet another family curse!

---

1 Corinthians 12:28 - "And God hath set some in the church, first apostles, secondarily prophets, thirdly teachers, after that miracles, then gifts of healings, helps, governments, diversities of tongues."

---

# 11

## *Alienation*

*"We are living in dystopia, in a world that is dominated by technology and disconnect, alienation, loneliness, and dysfunction."*

STEVEN WILSON

CURRENTLY, TWO OF OUR CHILDREN do not speak to us, and this breaks my heart. The relationship with the third child has been mended and it is going swimmingly. Because of the abuse I suffered, and my "No's" not being listened to, I try not to violate the boundaries our children placed upon us to stay out of their lives.

Our three children have at some time, either via text, message or chat message have said, "If this is what Christians are like then I want nothing to do with them," and "Stay out of my life." Well, if those are not clear enough boundaries, I do not know what they are.

In our defense, I was being a parent and saying no to their offensive behavior and manipulative demands. That was the response we got. At this time, it has been over fifteen years and just over six years since we have had any contact.

It is the sad truth, and it is not how we wish for things to be, but it is really their choice. They were treating us disrespectfully and making manipulative terroristic demands.

The ridiculous demands that were made were: to purchase a car, cell phone and an MP3 player for one child. The MP3 player was purchased but we were told it wasn't the one she wanted. We found out there was a young girl at the church we attended that didn't have a Christmas and guess what her request was? We happily gifted her the whole package, including the MP3 player, gift cards to load it with and extra gift cards for clothes. I stated directly that we would not be purchasing a car nor a cell phone as we had not purchased these items for the older children. I thought it was the end of the conversation, but it was just the tip of the iceberg. The attitude in the household became hostile, rude and unmanageable. We would ask for chores they had done previously to be done and they complained or asked why their dad could not do them. We later found out that they were being told that they did not need to listen to me as I was, "just their step-mom." At the present age, I think they knew better.

Life felt like I was constantly walking on eggshells, or more like land mines. I literally felt like I was going to have a heart attack. I came home early from work one day not feeling well. When I came in, I heard in a harsh and hateful voice, "What are you doing here?" I was not feeling well and snapped back, "I do not feel well, and this is my house." I then went to be and cried. This was breaking my heart.

This became the catalyst for the next few weeks. George and I had many conversations about the behavior and that I was not going to be able to hang on much longer with the anger, hostility and rudeness. The following Friday evening we met out into the living room for a family meeting. We were met with the crossed arms over the chest, looking down and not even participating. We got our point across, even if it did not really change anything.

From that day on, we had asked to be respected or we were going to ask for them to move out. The awful behavior continued for several more weeks, even though we were checking in on Fridays, nothing had changed. The time came when It was obvious that nothing was going to get better. We met again on a Friday evening and since there was no witnessed change in the behavior, we suggested that they move. Now, suddenly they were ready to converse. We were asked, "Where will I go? Why are you doing this to me?" From there it became a blame game, we were horrible parents. We did not give what was needed, and we would not drive or pay for things that were wanted etc. I refused to do these things while I was being treated so poorly and I don't give in to demands. Demands are a tactic of terrorists. Sadly I felt terrorized in our home once again.

A few years ago we received a phone call from the alienating child due to the prompting of her grandfather. I instantly thought that it was not heartfelt and suggested hanging up. Instantly it was said that they had thought about calling many times over the years, but just did not have the words (to say I'm sorry). To me it is as simple as, "I am sorry for my behavior and I retract the statement that has kept you from contacting me."

Another hurtful and disappointing event was when someone stole all the attention and caused unnecessary drama on Mother's Day by announcing that they were gay. It is a day that is supposed to be about the mother. I will be honest, as a christian I wasn't happy. BUT I love my children and George and I both accepted their decision and attended the wedding party, held at a gay bar in a near city. We actually had a lot of fun!

After a while things seemed fine. Sadly, their behavior changed, and this person was no longer the gentle, kind, loving young person we all knew, loved and adored. They became hostile, volatile, rude and uncaring. These were things that they were never like before. They were choosing to be rude to me and a few other family members. We had a conversation about the inappropriate behavior and our expectations. They became angry, hostile and left our home to live with my mother. After that things deteriorated very quickly, as they always did when mother was involved. My mother and her minions were a huge contributor to the alienation of our children. Whenever they talked to her or the others their pat answer was, "Oh, you are right, she IS a mean mom."

Due to my mother's declining health, there was a care conference planned. She had been deteriorating for some time. It was decided to proceed with comfort care measures. We were then told that she would pass in the next couple of days. After leaving mom's room and saying my final good-bye, a family member was standing against the wall and reached to me for comfort. I went around them and went towards the remainder of my family in the waiting room. Sadly, they were angry with me for not rushing to their side and comforting them. I felt like I honored their request to stay out of their life, even though I wanted to comfort them. I will be waiting forever for them to decide to retract their statements and apologize. Sadly, I have quit hoping that it will ever happen. Our home was once again turned into a war zone and my heart was the casualty.

The shortest alienation has been repaired. I said to George that if she ever comes around, she would not be allowed in our home. I had it in my mind that we would meet at a restaurant where we know groups of people will be and where we will be safe. All-of-a-sudden, there was a Facebook Messenger notification asking George why he was friends with her ex-husband and not her. He answered that he had no intention of being friends with anyone who was spreading vicious lies about us. At that moment she apologized and said that she missed us, and he said, "Thank you for apologizing, but I am not the person that you need to apologize to. You hurt your mom!" Then, not even three minutes later, I got a Facebook message apologizing and stating that we were missed and asked us for forgiveness. As weird as it seems, I totally was able to forgive.

The heart is a funny thing. I was so happy to have them all back in our lives. It was like the walls that I had built up just tumbled down as soon as they apologized. I am so glad. Relieved really! My heart is open to new possibilities. To date, we are doing fabulously well. We have made a point not to go without talking. We have had some hard conversations and we have done very well. We have both been able to say how we feel and how we have grown closer due to this. We have also decided that we will never do without each other again.

On Mother's Day I called and mentioned how proud I was of her and the mom that she had become. She said, "Thank you, but I am only the mom that I am because of the mom that you are to me."

During my childhood and adulthood, I also experienced alienation from my mother. If I made an opinion while we were talking on a phone call, she immediately disagreed and would hang up on me, sometimes not calling back for months on end. She would then call back out of the blue and act like nothing was wrong. If she was at our home, she would get all huffy, grab her stuff and leave again for weeks and even months on end. Then she would call and act like nothing had ever happened again. It was a vicious cycle. What she did not understand was; in those times (where we had no contact) I was happy, drama free and peaceful. The funniest part of this is that George would say, when she would finally call again, "Oh looks like she isn't mad anymore!"

My children will always be the best five things that have ever happened to me. Because of being alienated, I have formed many wonderful friendships with women who also have been alienated. Although being alienated is hard, we must always search for the silver lining in everything. I would have never made friends with these incredible women had it not been for our shared alienation/estrangement.

---

Job 19:19 - "All my inward friends abhorred me: and they whom I loved are turned against me."

---

# 12

$\sim H \sim$

## *The Wounded Heart Class*

*"I think that everybody, at one time or another, has been betrayed and lied to, and it's about the pain, and it's about the healing process, and it's about how do you get past that and move on."*

TINA KNOWLES

A FRIEND WHOM I LOVE VERY much was attending church with me one Sunday and there was mention of a class called "The Wounded Heart". Well, if that did not describe me, I do not know what did! So, I asked her if she would go with me to the class. She did not end up going, but instead paid for my book and the class for my birthday gift. I have never had a gift that shattered me, showed me where I was broken and helped me heal like this gift.

I truly and honestly never saw myself as shattered or even broken before this. I was. I was so shattered, broken, fragmented and even destroyed. I didn't even know how broken I was until I took this class. There is healing in being broken and allowing God to use it for His glory! There are also cracks in our brokenness so His light can shine and light the path of others along the way.

At this time, I also learned that music was something that brought back these feelings of remembrance. It is like you are rewinding a tape in your head of what you had gone through all over again. It shocks you as if someone had dumped a whole bucket of ice on your head. I learned what triggers were and that I actually had them. Three songs triggered me. Triggers can be music, smells, situations (seeing a past offender in public), places and people.

Our bodies are a complex operating system. We cannot ignore the triggers, symptoms and warnings it gives us. We must be aware that it is a package deal. There is our mental, physical, spiritual and emotional health to consider. Ignoring any part of this delicate system could result in disastrous results. Our bodies are very similar to a car. You put in gas/food and they have energy to run. We must take care of our bodies by listening to its incredibly unique needs. Some people ignore the mental and emotional side of our bodies. This could result in mental illness and depression as well as a myriad of other health conditions.

It hurt to go through this. It hurt for so many reasons. It hurt watching dear sisters tell their stories knowing the abuse that they had suffered as well. Opening up Pandora's box is tough, but there is healing when you allow God to direct it. True healing, beautiful and cleansing healing.

I stuck it out and felt completely wrecked as a result. My pain, anger, hatred, bitterness and poison was slowly leaving. This helped in so many ways. My PTSD (post-traumatic stress disorder) got better. I no longer tried to control things and situations, so I feel safe. I could now sit anywhere in a restaurant,

We live in an unsafe world. We can do all we can, but it is still an unsafe world. I am so much happier, feel safer and get over things so much quicker than before. I know I can only control me; what I do, think and feel, no more than that! That is my job! In the past, I was only able to sit against a wall and in a corner at a restaurant so that no one sneaks up on me. I needed to see fully around me so that I felt safe. If I could not find a seat that met these specifications, we left the restaurant.

I know peace now! I have been set free to enjoy life and live it to my best ability. The things that have brought me the most pain have also brought me the most change and exposed gifts, talents and abilities in me that I was never aware of before!

Mostly I feel sorry for the women who did not stick it out in "The Wounded Heart" class. They are still stuck in all that brokenness. They are probably choosing the same patterns as before and are not understanding why things do not and or will not change! They will never change until they examine the "Why". Until they open-up their soul and see what is causing it internally. It is that damage, brokenness, hurt and wound that has never healed. It is filled with pus; seeping and weeping over into your life, making you hurt. This causes you to be offended over things that are not even about you. You just get used to it, but it is keeping you from joy! True joy and happiness and from enjoying this life!

I believe that life has a way of cracking the lenses (as in eyeglasses) we look through. As life unfolds and we get hurt, abused, neglected, abandoned and wounded, the lenses of our life get cracked. This skews everything we look at and discolors everything we experience.

One of the things that I have noticed, prior to taking this course, is that I had all these feelings bumbling around inside and I had not known what to do with them. This kind of felt like a beehive buzzing inside of me at all times. This left me feeling like I was constantly juggling feelings and that they were going to be coming down and hitting me. You have two hands and feelings that are constantly moving. I did not have enough hands to catch them. It left me feeling helpless. I was out of control. I was overwhelmed.

After reading *The Wounded Heart* book and working through the chapters in the workbook, I was able to lay these feelings down where they made sense and where I felt they belonged. This gave me a sense of peace.

When children are going through these types of feelings, it is even more traumatic. They do not have the words to express what or how they are feeling about what has happened to them. They may find it difficult to describe. They are often afraid to speak up due to threats from the offenders. When we have these feelings, and we do not know where they go, we deal with guilt. They just stay inside rumbling around causing even more pain, frustration and anger. When we read *The Wounded Heart* Book and utilize the workbook by Dr. Dan B. Allender it gives us a step-by-step process for cleaning out these wounds and moving forward in our lives. It offers us a way to deal with and move through these painful emotions and gives us permission to leave them where they belong. As abused, broken and wounded people we don't know we have the power within ourselves to do this, to walk away from shame and the belief that we are broken and will remain there forever. It gives you permission to switch the blame from us to the perpetrator. It takes the weight off our shoulders and this is so freeing.

I now know how and what to do with feelings, emotions and how to take care of me. Despite what I have been through, done to myself or what others have done to me, I am now able to manage these feelings and emotions. I feel at peace, capable, willing and able. What a sense of peace this feeling brings.

---

Psalms 6:2 - "Have mercy upon me, O LORD; for I am weak: O LORD, heal me; for my bones are vexed."

---

# 13

## *Mother*

*"I think, at a child's birth, if a mother could ask a fairy godmother to endow it with the most useful gift, that gift should be curiosity."*

ELEANOR ROOSEVELT

WARNING: THIS IS THE RAW and a real side of my mother from my perspective.

She was a woman that many people supposedly knew and loved. I never quite understood what they saw in her. But then I saw a very different side to her.

When drama unfolds in or around my life, it reminds me of my mother. It makes me want to run away mentally, emotionally and physically. I just cannot, will not, be near, around or take part in it (the drama).

The truth is, neither of my parents were "good parents" and should not have had children but, if that were the case, I would not be here to tell my story.

I do not remember ever being hugged, kissed or shown affection by my mother. Looking back, I see I have issues with people in my space/bubble. Now I can show love and affection and allow people into my personal space. I have and do care very deeply for people! But it is a struggle. For example, if you are a hugger and you hold on past a small hug, I feel panicky and want to run. I need to really care on a personal level to want to touch you or allow you to touch me. This is my "bubble". I do not mind hugs if they are not holding on forever, and I can break away when I feel uncomfortable. Honestly, I thought I was broken for so long. In fact, I thought that I was incapable of love all together. As I grew older, I came to believe that it was my mother who was broken and unable to love.

There have been hundreds, maybe even thousands of times that I have wondered why I got the family that I did. I have always felt like the odd person out. Like I never fit into my family. Something would happen that everyone else would be ok with, but I was not. I felt like this a lot. I would see things that my conscience would be triggered by. I would wonder why others would be ok with it. I just knew that I could not be bought enough to let these things happen. When I started to speak up, again it was obvious that I was the only one who felt this way. As mother would always say things like, "Stay out of it! It has nothing to do with you! Mind your own business!" Those were her usual statements.

Our relationship was always filled with strife. As I grew older it just seemed to magnify. I did not allow her to live vicariously through me. I did not want to go to the prom, dances or be a debutante at the ball (sarcasm intended). I did things the hard way, the honest way. I was fair, truthful, helping and caring. I let people in my bubble and still do.

Mom had her bubble and if you did not think, behave and believe like her, you were not in her bubble! Our bubbles only touched in one place, ever so slightly. Honestly, I sometimes even wonder if we were even related. Quite honestly, I truly wondered if I was the result of my mother being raped by her prior boyfriend and then my dad just taking me in as his child. I researched to see that I came along promptly ten months after their wedding.

As I look back, I really felt like Disney's character Cinderella. My mother was the evil stepmom. There were always excuses for why I had to do the chores. I was the "scullery maid". The one big difference was that I did not get the pleasure of going to the ball, leaving a glass slipper and getting "prince charming" and I was far from living in an immaculate castle.

I learned that gifts came with strings and they were used as bribery later when she wanted something. She always wanted me to do something that I was uncomfortable with and the cost was too uncomfortable (lie, keep secrets, look the other way, keep my mouth shut). Promises meant nothing when they came from her and the "I love you" statements were just something she said when she hung up the phone. These gifts were not gifts to me.

When I stopped accepting her offerings, because I would not be manipulated or bribed, the estrangement became more frequent and for longer time periods. Statements from her included: "Why are you like this?" or, "What did I ever do to deserve this treatment?" or, "You ungrateful child, I should go adopt some Down syndrome children. They would not treat me like this! You kids are driving me to the insane asylum."

There were many family friends who had young daughters that mother took under her wing and showed preference for and showered with gifts and affection. She always seemed to mention how kind and how adoring they behaved towards her.

I embarrassed my mother when I opened the big "family secret". I explained that someone that we knew was raping and molesting children and that he attempted to touch me. Not to mention, the big one, when I became an unwed mother at the early age of seventeen.

The day that mom officially found out that I was pregnant, I was in school and had gotten sick, so the teacher sent me to the guidance counselors office. While waiting for her, one of my classmates said, "I heard that you were pregnant, what are you going to do?" I told her that I was going to keep my baby. Behind me the guidance counselor and another teacher said (I am not sure which one), "I think that you are ruining a grade A student's life and that you should get an abortion." I replied back, "How is this ruining a grade A student's life when he left, and I am stuck with a baby? Furthermore, it is none of your (expletive) business." They then sent me to the principal's office where he was waiting for me where he stated, "I heard the teachers and guidance counselors' side of the story and I would like to hear yours!"

I recounted my side of the story. He asked what I planned to do, and I told him that I was checking myself out of school to raise my baby.

Either the guidance counselor or the assistance principal called my mother to come and get me. At the same time, she had also gotten a call from my siblings' school that she was not feeling well also. We were headed to get her when my mother had me captive. She had noticed that some sanitary pads were not being used and she said, "Is there something that you would like to tell me?" I said, "I think that I might be pregnant." Then mom flipped out in her usual way while driving and I said to her, "Mom, if you do not put your hands back on the wheel, I may not stay pregnant," as the car began to veer towards an oncoming farm truck. She then composed herself and we went to get my sibling.

Right after this news, she hurried out to find me a husband. I distinctly remember her saying the one she found would be a good husband once we sobered him up, though she denied initially saying this.

Another way that I embarrassed my mother was when a friend of hers arrived at the house after hearing that mother was going to be a grandma too. The first thing that came out of her mouth was, "I hear that you are going to have a unwed grandchild just like all of mine." This infuriated me. I fired off, "I don't ever want to hear of you speaking this way to my child or your grandchildren in my presence. I do not understand why children are left to bear the burden of shame when it is their parents that left them. Why aren't the parents labeled instead of the child?" Mother looked at me with this shock and disbelief. Once again, I disappointed her.

Sadly, mother and I were never close. I learned a lot from her. Unfortunately, it was all the things I did not want to be. As soon as she learned I had an opinion and that I felt differently than she did at the age of twelve, it was pretty much all over between us.

Happily, I can inform you that I am not broken! I love very quickly and deeply then sometimes later find out that this person is not deserving of my love. I end up being disappointed once again. I temporarily close off until I am healed, process the situation and then build my strength to try again. I can never go back to that dark cave that I had put myself in long ago.

I do believe that my mother was broken though. I do believe that she did not know how to love and sadly that included herself as well.

We all have the choice if we repeat the bad decisions of our parents. Hopefully, we do not! Due to how my mother played favorites with my siblings, this is one of the main reasons why I choose to treat all our children equally. Even if that very thing caused one of our children to alienate us. Our birth and stepchildren were all treated the same. All equally! I chose not to ignore things that were technically not my business (as mother said repeatedly throughout my life), especially if it was abuse or wrong. I got involved and tried to help. Yes, it hurts, all these choices hurt in one way or another.

I choose to believe that helping, even when It goes wrong, is better than hiding and carrying it inside you for all those years as my aunt, mother and grandmother did. I also believe that the knowledge of the problem or situation will eventually hurt you from the inside out with guilt and cause mental and physical, emotional and even sexuall health problems if it is not dealt with.

Regrettably, I do not remember a time when I felt loved by my mother or I felt love for her. This was mainly from the age of twelve forward. I have not missed her since she passed away. I did not ever learn to respect her because she gave that away to my dad. She was always making him do her dirty work. She would cry and lay guilt trips on us to get her way. Then the guilt she would mount became even worse. It was at this point that I no longer accepted that guilt. I was outside of her bubble while others fought for the scraps of love that she would throw their way.

I learned so much after my mother passed away. So many people came up to me and asked if I ever wondered why they left our life. Then they would explain why. Some of the stories shocked me and some did not. I knew my mother was greedy, selfish and a social climbing snob. Many people have said that my mother no longer wanted to be their friends when she found out that their husbands made more money than my dad did. When I told her about the molestation, instead of talking to the parents of the men who abused me, she just refused to answer their calls or have anything to do with them.

Shortly after dad passed, she told me that she married beneath her class when she married my father. I was furious! How dare she? I will never forget one time, dad and I had been out running errands and he looked at me with haunted hurt eyes and said, "Did you know how many credit cards she has in my name?" Oh, my heart broke for him. He loved her so much and to this day I still do not understand why.

I also learned how much she preferred my siblings over myself. After mother died I was informed that mother said she did not want me to inherit anything. I was also told that there were people telling family members who would listen that I had stolen their inheritance. Mom had requested to split up her jewelry so that all the children, grandchildren and great grandchildren got their birth stones from her mother and grandmother's rings.

To this day no one knows where this jewelry has gone, but we know who had it last. One of the last fights between mom and I was over her bank cards. My siblings were constantly using her money because they had access to her bank account through bank cards. I told her that she needed to get her cards back so she could use her money. She screamed at me stating that I was jealous and asked if I wanted a card! I screamed back, "No"! She looked at me and said, "Why not?" I said, "When your money comes up missing it will never be me that is in question." Sadly, several people rode on her queenly robe for the twelve years after dad passed away.

I cannot imagine how it feels to not have to work for the things that you want. My mother was so selfish and spoiled. She was living off others and others were living off her. That is not who I am. I chose to be a truth teller, to work hard, be honest and have integrity like my father.

Sadly, I am still processing my mother and our relationship. I am working through this relationship or lack of it to this day. I learn more every day and bring up memories that are more difficult with the intent to heal.

During this time with my mother, I felt like I was invisible. After I turned twelve, I lived in the home but was not considered part of the family, just the maid and servant.

When she was dying, lying slumping in the hospital bed, she looked like an unwanted "dolly" that someone had thrown away. At this time, I felt sorry for and pitied her because she never really loved herself either.

All I know is I am sitting here trying to understand and heal the "mother wound" she left me with. I see another book in my future, the wounds life gives us and how to deal with them.

---

Exodus 20:12 - "Honor thy father and thy mother: that thy days may be long upon the land which the LORD thy God giveth thee."

---

# 14

❦

# *My Daddy, My Hero*

*"My Daddy was my hero. He was always there for me when I needed him. He listened to me and taught me so many things. But most of all he was fun."*

BINDI IRWIN, DAUGHTER TO STEVE IRWIN, "CROCODILE HUNTER"

DADDY, OH, HOW I MISS him. I wonder what he and our lives would be like if he were still here. I would be taking care of Uncle Ed and think, "Oh my goodness what if dad were here, the adventures we would have. Fun, yes, we would have fun and mischief!

Whenever daddy would come home from a shift where we were awake, I would run and hug him and smell the smell of the mill. I remember smelling sulfur. It was not the greatest smell in the world, but it meant that my daddy was home. It was a comforting smell because then I knew that sanity had returned to home.

I miss his strong truth, his willingness to help, his sense of humor and his joy.

I will not lie, he was mean - a lot. He was abusive and there were a lot of explosions, yelling, hitting and "poking" (literal poking to the chest and forehead). There would be name calling and hurtful things flung at us. He would say that he wished he had never had kids or that he wished he could send us kids to the far corners of the earth so we wouldn't fight. He was frustrated and did not understand. I am not making excuses or saying any of this was right. I am not negating any of the bad. I know how much the things he said hurt, as well as the spankings we did not deserve.

The main difference between my mother and father was that my father tried to do better than what was done for him. His out-bursts would embarrass mom. She would say, "Oh Joseph!"

Honestly, I do not think that my dad knew that my mom pitted us against one another. We would try to get along, thereafter fighting for whatever scraps my mom threw our way. I do not know if my dad ever truly knew my mom until he was dying, and it broke his and my heart.

But there was another side to him as well. He had a heart of gold. He was a very good man. He was honest and hard working. You would always know where he stood with things and where you stood with him. This earned my respect for sure.

He was so sweet to us as girls. He always told us how pretty we were and that we did not need all that "war paint" on our faces. He always made us feel beautiful. He genuinely cared, was a helper and was really, truly a good man. He loved Jesus with all his heart. When he was dying, I asked him if he was scared, and he said, "No, I'm not going to see Jesus and all those who went before me." Oh, he was so brave! That must be where I get my bravery from! One time my aunt accused my dad of being just like her ex, the pedophile. Everyone got all up in arms about it...they fired back insults and added to the drama. Not me. I simply messaged her and said, do not ever message me things like this again. I have no problem never speaking to you again. I hate drama and that was all she was trying to do, make everyone miserable just like she was.

I do not know what my dad saw in mother, but I surely think he deserved better than her. He worked so hard for all of us. He was always helping others; he really would have given the shirt off his back if he needed to! He did not speak much, but when he did it was short, sweet and valuable.

Sadly, I learned the most about him while I was caring for him while he was dying of cancer. We have very few pictures of daddy because he was working so much or working outside or helping others. I do cherish the pictures I do have of him. I have scrapbooked most of them with fishing pages because he loved fishing so much.

When dad finally got the diagnosis of asbestosis cancer, we were all pretty shaken up. I will never forget how mom, many family members, and George and I were just mortified. We all piled into a huddle and bawled. Not my dad! He got up and walked out. I chased after him asking him what he was doing, He replied, ``I am going fishing. You heard the doctor. Do all you can and want to do until you can't anymore." He did, right up to two days before he passed. It was on a Tuesday evening that he went to bed then was comatose until Friday morning when he passed.

I tell you, the doctors, nurses and hospice workers all said what an exemplary man he was. Most people hear the word cancer and lay down to die from that moment on, but not my daddy.

When I took care of my uncle, daddy's brother, I learned even more about my father, his brother and their childhood. They were both shuffled around in foster homes, group and boy homes, for most of their young life. Eventually they were separated.

I learned a terrible and sad thing too. My daddy was one of the front-line men who had to shoot at women and children strapped with explosives or lose his very own life and those of his comrades in war. What a terrible and tragic thing to have to live with, but Daddy never spoke of this. My daddy truly was and always will be my hero.

Every year for Christmas dad would make "gag gifts". One year, dad made me a bra out of Cool Whip containers. It was two containers connected in the center with rope. He used this as a way for me to come to grips, or to desensitize me from the way that boys might treat me due to being large breasted. It was not at all sexual in nature when he did this.

Early on when I was having my menstrual cycle, I figured out that I was out of pads. So, I went to go ask my dad when my mom was going to be home because she was working at the time. I ended up asking him a couple of times. He ended up asking me if I had run out of pads. This floored me. The answer was obviously, "Yes". He took me to the store, and I thought that he was just going to hand me some money and stay in the car in the parking lot. No…he went in, while we were in the aisle, he proceeded to talk loudly that I did not use tampons but pads. He reached out for the type that we used saying, "Isn't this the brand you use?" and put the package under his arm and proceeded to walk to the register. He placed it on the conveyor belt in line and the cashier asked if we needed a bag, he said, "No" and put the package under his arm and we walked out. I literally sat there in the car and wondered who he was and what had happened to my dad? On the way home he had explained that he had been with my mother all these years and knew about women's cycles and that it was pretty obvious that I had run out of sanitary napkins. My daddy will always be my hero.

Genesis 31:5 - "And He said unto them, I see your father's countenance, that it is not toward me as before; but the God of my father hath been with me."

# 15

## *Choosing to Be Different Than What I Knew*

*"I realized that my strength was being different."*

BETSEY JOHNSON

THERE WERE MANY DIFFERENCES BETWEEN the way my parents raised us and the way I parented my children. I was able to learn a new way, a way in which I would have loved to have been treated by my parents. I took any and every parenting class that was offered and even repeated many times every year.

My parents, God rest their souls, were not good parents. Sometimes I struggle with this. I struggle with the whys or the why nots. It is sad that I can empathize with my dad but not with my mom. I saw that he at least tried to do better than his parents did for him! He pursued and held a job he hated, even though we all paid for it, to support us. It was important for him to provide a decent, safe running car, a roof over our heads, food in our bellies and clothes on our backs because he did not have that as a child!

The way they talked to us children (or at us) is where I learned to be different. I did not say terrible things to them. I would never tell my children that their opinion, which my dad always said, would back-fire on me. It never has. I wanted my children to feel valued, important, loved and wanted. These were all things I did not feel from my parents!

My children learned respect without fear. Not at first, but after I learned of these new ways to parent, they did. At first, I was distant and cold and dictatorial like my dad and emotionally absent like my mom. With the parenting classes I learned to be firm, but loving, understanding, supportive and encouraging, but my kids knew I meant business. They knew that I am not the bad guy but if they ever needed a reason to say no, I would be it. That was helpful with their father and with peer pressure. I wanted them to know I was there for them, but If they ever misused that, they knew I was there to bust their butts. They trusted that I would take the fall if they were ever uncomfortable.

We had code words set up. All they had to do to activate it, if they were out, with friends or family and they felt unsafe, scared or fearful, was say the code words and mom was on it.

I learned so much about what not to do parenting wise from my parent's example. But I was able to turn a lot of these bad choices around to be a good example and a good mom for our kids.

For a long time, I felt like I could never do better than my dad did for us. Then I realized-yes, I could and did. Financially this would be hard to obtain, though money doesn't solve every problem. It turns out that there is more value in a life changed than monetary gains.

I have spoken to my boys and said, "I am sorry for so much of your childhood". I was thinking they were going to bomb me, and they did not. They said, "What are you talking about mom? We felt loved, we didn't know we were poor, and you were always there for us."

I felt so relieved to hear this. To know I made the right choices and changes for our children.

I had called our daughter on Mother's Day and told her how proud we were of her and the mother she has become to our granddaughters. Her reply was, "I am only the mother that I am to my daughters because of the mother that you were to me." That was an amazing feeling.

I have always felt different all of my life. Learning to change the things I never liked seemed far easier than being untrue to myself. That square peg in a round hole type of thing. An oddity, rare, different, special, strange, peculiar, unique and therefore precious. It's so funny that many people say these things in a negative connotation, whereas I see them in a totally different light. I see these traits as a positive thing. I am proud of these traits, talents and abilities. I no longer fear and or worry about what others think of my differences, talents or abilities. I have worked hard to attain and maintain them! I have learned to accept, embrace and love each and every facet of who I am, what made me that way and who I am becoming. That includes all the abuse, neglect and the people who perpetrated it against me. I am a better "me" for having gone through it all and came out the other end an amazing person (whether others agree or not, I believe it).

---

Deuteronomy 14:2 - "For thou art a holy people unto the LORD thy God, and the LORD hath chosen thee to be a peculiar people unto himself, above all the nations that are upon the earth."

---

# 16

## *Safety*

*"I am thankful the most important key in history was invented. It's not the key to your house, your car, your boat, your safety deposit box, your bike lock or your private community. It's the key to order, sanity, and peace of mind. The key is 'Delete.'"*

ELAYNE BOOSLER

I NEVER FELT SAFE AT HOME, both during my childhood, my first marriage or when I lived with my long-term boyfriend/high school sweetheart. So naturally one of my main goals as I aged, and especially after my first marriage, was to make sure that our home was a safe zone. Sadly, we have allowed some people over the years to stay with us that have threatened that safety. This included both family and friends. We have also lost some relationships because I have had to take back the helm of our home and regain our safety, sanctity and peace that we strove so hard to attain.

Also, I have realized that safety is not always possible. We live in a very fallen world. We can only do what we can to feel safe and keep ourselves out of unsafe situations. We may still feel unsafe.

In 1989 my boys and I went to a movie theatre and my boys told me that they had to go to the bathroom. After they had been to the restroom, the boys explained that there was a creepy man staring at them. Because of my past sexual abuse, my children were well versed in what to do if something happened to them. They also used the buddy system if I could not go into the bathroom with them. We found out the following day exactly who that creepy man was. We later found out that it was Wesley Allan Dodd (serial killer and sex offender). I was extremely thankful and grateful that my children were not his victim. He had sexually assaulted and murdered three young boys in Washington.

At the age of thirteen, Dodd began exposing himself to children in his neighborhood. His father eventually told an Oregon newspaper that he was aware of the boy's behavior but largely ignored it, since he felt his son was otherwise, "A well-behaved child who never had problems with drugs, drinking, or smoking." By the time he entered high school, Dodd had progressed to molestation, beginning with his younger cousins, and then neighborhood children he offered to babysit, as well as the children of a woman his father was dating. At the age of 15 Dodd was arrested for indecent exposure, but police released him with recommendation of juvenile counseling.

"On November 13, 1989, Dodd attempted to abduct a 6-year-old child from the restroom of the Liberty Theatre in Camas, Washington (the day after our visit to the theatre), but the child began fighting and crying as Dodd was leaving the theater through the lobby, carrying the boy in his arms. Despite Dodd's attempts to calm the boy, theater employees became suspicious. Once outside, Dodd released his victim before getting into his car driving away. The boyfriend of the boy's mother, William 'Ray' Graves, came to the theater lobby and was told that the boy had nearly been abducted. Graves went outside the theater in the direction where Dodd was last seen. Dodd's car had broken down a short distance away from the theater and he was attempting to start the motor. In order not to raise Dodd's suspicion and to stall for time, Graves offered to help him. He then put Dodd into a headlock and brought him back to the theater, where employees called the police.

After pleading guilty to the charges of murder, Dodd received the death penalty. Dodd was executed by hanging at 12:05 a.m. on January 5, 1993 at Washington State Penitentiary." Wikipedia

Also around this time we allowed a friend and my ex husband's co worker to move in with his wife and their three small boys. I had a weird feeling I was being lied to, but kept it under wraps. Later that night I went to the refrigerator where she placed a bunch of medicine and looked at the label which confirmed my feelings. Her children had head lice, a really really bad case of it. Mostly because she hadn't used the medicine and treated them. They were missing hair in huge patches and had scabs and sores. I confronted her in the morning and we went on a cleaning binge. It turns out she had never known what to do, but I quickly showed her how to treat this.

One thing I have found is, I will always be safe in the arms of Jesus, God and His Holy Spirit. That gives me peace!

I also hate drama. There have been many times when people staying in our home have brought plenty of that.

I have issues with strange people parading through our home. There have been times when our roommates have allowed others to come over to our house after we were asleep. I have gotten up in the night only to come face to face with someone I did not know. This was very unsettling.

Once I felt unsafe when I felt a breeze going through the house that awoke me at three a.m. I found my front door wide open with one person inside the house while the other partner was outside pacing and acting like he was on drugs.

I have given refuge to friends only to have them sleep with my ex-husband, lie and break my heart.

We have had family that have used us, pretty much until we were at risk to lose all that we had worked for several times. All this and I am the bad guy when I have finally taken enough and take back the helm of our home and life. I will protect our home at any-and-all costs. Sadly, I am getting to where I no longer ever want to offer the key to our door to anyone ever again.

---

Leviticus 25:18 - "Wherefore ye shall do my statutes, and keep my judgments, and do them; and ye shall dwell in the land in safety."

---

# 17

## *Momma Jo*

*"To be a mother is a beautiful thing, but to be able to assume the role for a child in need is nothing less than amazing. I believe that any woman who takes on the role of a mother, whether it be naturally or through foster care or adoption, should be held in the highest regard."*

### RAHEEM DeVAUGHN

W E MET WHEN I WAS working at a hair salon right after I had graduated from beauty school. When the full-time girls were on vacation, I would take care of their clients.

We were sitting at the nail table and Jo said, " (Sofia, can I be honest with you?" I said "Yes", feeling scared and ever so excited. She said, "Ever since I met you, I have felt kind of strong feelings for you, like a mother feels for her children. Is that ok?" I said, "Yes", I too have felt that way." She said it was kind of like I was her daughter. We started spending time together, having lunches and talking and laughing. This is when I started calling her "Momma Jo" and she referred to me as her daughter.

Years passed and we always kept track of one other. She moved but she was only gone for a few years. When she came back, she had lost my Information. She went to see our mutual friend at the salon, who was like one of my older sisters (after all it felt like family there) and asked her if she knew where she could find me. She laughed and pointed right across the street to where I was working at that time!

When Jo arrived at the classroom I worked in, I was in the other building and they called me and told me that someone was here to see me. Not thinking, I walked over and when I saw her, I started to cry. We both exclaimed loudly how much we had missed each other and hugged while we cried happy tears. We exchanged contact information and never lost track again. Lunches and even dinners resumed, and George and I went to visit her frequently. I loved that woman more than most people could ever understand.

One time she cupped her hands around my face and kissed me on the forehead as we were leaving. I started to cry, and she said, "Did I hurt you?" I explained that my mother had never kissed me or touched me like that! She never hugged me or held me closely either (my mom).

To this day I struggle with physical touch, but I sure cherished Momma Jo's kiss! We both love sunflowers! To know that someone you love and care about so much shares something that you love too was very special. I have two sunflower items she gave me, a big jug with four sunflowers and eucalyptus, another with foliage, and a basket with sunflower printed fabric inside. I cherish these as well. I have grown sunflowers nearly every year in her honor.

Momma Jo was firm and honest, stubborn and had a sense of humor. I loved her laugh! I also loved how she would constantly remind me to wear my sunscreen. To me it was like her saying I love you, so take care of yourself.

As George and I were leaving the cremation place after my mother had died, I can't even remember if I called her or she called me, but I told her I wasn't going to go to mother's funeral service. She informed me that I was going, and I would do so because I was her daughter and that I would honor her because that is who I am. I went, but I wanted to flee screaming with everything inside of me.

I ignored the lies that were delivered through the officiant of the funeral. I was treated like a street urchin that wandered in from the slums for food. I wanted to scream, shout and tell everyone the truth. But I knew no one would listen. So, I sat through the entire ceremony seething even though I never loved or respected my mother, I still needed to honor her wishes. I am so thankful for my friends who went with me as they are more like family than my immediate family ever were.

I realized that Momma Jo showed me so much. She showed me how loving a "real" mother could be even though this was far from the truth in the natural.

Sadly, as we were headed to her home to see her, I found out that she had been in the hospital and had passed away. My heart was truly broken. I did get the chance to attend her funeral and for that I was very thankful. Thankful that I had known and loved her. Better yet, I knew that she loved me as well. Momma Jo was a wonderful, strong, opinionated and caring woman. Momma Jo blessed me with smiles, joy and a beautiful feeling of being loved.

---

Exodus 2:10 - "And the child grew, and she brought him unto Pharaoh's daughter, and he became her son. And she called his name Moses: and she said, because I drew him out of the water."

---

# 18

Dedication and Loyalty

*"Success is about dedication. You may not be where you want to be or do what you want to do when you're on the journey. But you've got to be willing to have vision and foresight that leads you to an incredible end."*

USHER

I HAVE WORKED AT AN ORGANIZATION in which I believed in its values, mission and how much it helped people. People like me and my family. At first, I volunteered until a friend said some magical words, "Sofia, they aren't going to create a job for you, you need to apply!" I cannot even tell you who it was that said that, but I applied for a job as a nutrition services aide. A cook! This was something I learned I could do very well as a result of having hungry boys to feed. I did that for a year or two and then moved into a classroom aide position for more hours and benefits! I loved this position until a parent attacked me when I was working with her and her child on a performance review.

I found out later that she was a meth addict and that was why she apparently took what I said wrong, even though my teachers said I was doing marvelously. I then applied and was accepted at the administration offices for the procurement specialist position. I filled that role for fourteen years. I was a staff member for seventeen years and a volunteer for ten. I was there twenty-seven years total.

I think the reason I stayed so long is because I felt I owed the agency for saving our lives. Mostly, I am so sad that the agency no longer represents what it did when my children and I were in the program. We had counseling, parenting and education classes and you could earn early childhood education credits through taking the classes!

I was able to teach some classes on couponing and how to save money. It was a beautiful program. I loved working there until some changes made it unbearable to continue. I still feel so blessed to have worked with some of the finest and most amazing coworkers/friends ever!

Under the teaching of two very brilliant and gifted supervisors I thrived in my position. They understood how I operated, and they utilized my strengths and played down my weaknesses. They always found ways for me to choose opportunities for growth in this field that came down to signing up for extracurricular activities, classes and regular testing to keep me on my toes. I loved this job. I accelerated at it. They gave me the opportunity to work in safety and I bravely created the "green team". This included working in research, finding unsafe chemicals, instituted recycling at administration offices and later out to all our outlying sites. Through this endeavor, I learned a lot about toxic chemicals that are in our cleaning supplies. As a result of this, I was able to reason this out that these chemicals were in our personal care products. I chose to increase my knowledge on my own time and I learned about an Essential Oil company called Young Living and I have diligently pursued this in my personal life. I really love knowing that the products I'm using are not going to further harm me, my family and my pets.

Unfortunately, I was accused of theft and an investigation was lobbied against me. The result of the investigation was inconclusive. For two years I was treated as a guilty imbecile, utter and complete moron. I quit when I realized I was on the brink of committing suicide. Upon this contemplation, I promptly went home and talked to my husband and told him how I was feeling and told him that I wanted to quit. He agreed that this was what I needed to do. Honestly and sadly the only reason I did not commit suicide was that our dog would not understand why his momma had not returned home.

I spoke to a person in human resources and asked about the best route to take and was advised to utilize the family emergency medical leave act.

That program was only for thirty days. I knew then that I could not and would not return, so I drafted my resignation letter.

On the last day of the month, I went in, asked for the human resources manager and said that I was there to resign. I was asked if I was sure. I said, "Absolutely, positively (with a smile on my face)!" I then asked for a copy of my resignation, signed as proof of receipt. I waited while the document was signed, copied and returned to me. I was then told "I guess there is nothing left to say but, good luck on your future endeavors." and held out their hand to shake. I shook it and smiled and then turned and walked out the door. I was sad that my career had ended this way. But I felt a ten ton weight lifted off my shoulders knowing I would never be abused, mistreated, ignored, criticized or any of the other myriad of feelings and emotions I had been feeling for those two years. Quite honestly it has taken four years to heal from this experience. To be able to drive by without looking at the building without thinking hateful and bad thoughts. Knowing that there is the One who knows that I would have never stolen from anyone, let alone a company who helped me so much. The people who did this to me, obviously never knew the integrity of the woman they mistreated. They will never understand who and what they let go when they pushed me to the edge. Most of all, they lost out on all the things they never knew about me. I was the blessing they drove away and that is truly sad. I would like to be clear, I only had 3 bad supervisors there. The REST were completely amazing! And I still believe the agency is good, just had some bad apples in higher up positions that were ruining what it stood for. BUT again, That's not my karma.

Matthew 25:23 - "His lord said unto him, Well done, good and faithful servant; thou hast been faithful over a few things, I will make thee ruler over many things: enter thou into the joy of thy lord."

# 19

Marriage

*"Chains do not hold a marriage together. It is threads, hundreds of tiny threads, which sew people together through the years."*

SIMONE SIGNORET

WHEN GEORGE AND I GOT together I was pretty wounded, bitter and broken. I think he also was broken and wounded as a result of a lot of family and past relationship situations. These types of woundings cause a lot of misunderstanding, disagreements and even more problems in the marriage. Even more so when we are unaware of how badly hurt we are. George and I have been together for over twenty-five years. Though it has not been perfect, it has been rough, tough, hard and even really, really bad at times. It has also been really good. He is my rock. He keeps me from floating away in my dreams, but he also allows me space to grow, change and keep on dreaming. He is so kind, gentle and understanding,

We raised all our five children as though they were ours. Sometimes we threatened that we would like to sell them. There have been many instances when I doubted his love. It is hard for me to believe his words when I have found out some of the incredibly hurtful and dumb things he has done. George's dad taught him that lying is something that is acceptable in a relationship.

My father-in-law hid many things from my mother in law, and she hid many things from him. I told George that I will not live that way. Lying is not a way of life I want to encourage, support or endorse. It took quite a while before George understood this and it almost cost us our marriage many times.

He has always been kind, listened and supported all my dreams and weird ideas. He truly has been my anchor in this ocean called life. The hardest part has been in having trust issues. He has been aware of this and has risked losing my trust for some of the things he has knowingly and repeatedly done. Although, he truly has been the kindest man I know.

When I think back over the years, he has never lifted a hand towards me, said a mean or loud word to me or been unkind. He truly has been a gentleman in all forms of the word.

Ever since the beginning George has been there for my boys and I, even when the boys were being little creeps. He has truly embraced us. It is a beautiful thing when two people come together to unite and blend two families. I personally think we did very well and were it not for outside influences we would have been exceptional.

I often feel like the song by Bette Midler, "Wind Beneath My Wings" is an appropriate description for our marriage. I'm the eagle and George is the wind beneath my wings.

---

Genesis 2:24 - "Therefore shall a man leave his father and his mother and shall cleave unto his wife: and they shall be one flesh."

---

# 20

Foster Parenting

*"It's not the word before parent that defines, but rather the love and dedication in the parent's heart."*

ADOPTION.COM

SHORTLY AFTER GEORGE AND I got married, we found out that a family member's children were placed into foster care. We decided together with our children (as a family) that we would apply to be foster parents. This was with the intent of getting our relatives out of the foster care system and with family.

We went through the classes and the process. We got all the way through to the final investigation which was the home visit. We thought that everything went so well. We thereafter received a letter that we had been denied because, "My kitchen was unsanitary, and our dogs were aggressive and unkept (though the dogs were never seen by the investigator)." The "unsanitary" part of the kitchen was because we were missing two lower cabinet doors where our pots and pans and large bowls were kept. Because of the dogs, the hair could get in this area and this was "unsanitary". The doors were downstairs being refinished and would have been installed prior to the children arriving. The third reason was that we had made two bedrooms in the attic space. The pitch of the roof was "too steep" although a grown man could stand up in the center.

The children ended up going to their father. We were not part of their life until they were able to seek us out on their own.

We were deeply grieved that we were treated so unfavorably. We are happily able to report that we have a close relationship with our nieces and nephews.

To this day I feel like my nieces and nephews are just my bonus children and I love them as much as our children. I would never dream of sabotaging or speaking ill or encouraging them to alienate their parents, as their parents have done to my children.

Romans 8:15 - "For ye have not received the spirit of bondage again to fear; but ye have received the Spirit of adoption, whereby we cry, Abba, Father."

# 21

*Betrayal*

*"Betrayal can be extremely painful, but it's up to you how much that pain damages you permanently."*

EMILY V. GORDON

I F ANYONE HAD A REASON to stay bitter, broken and wounded, I think It was me. After all the sexual, physical, mental and emotional abuse, misuse, neglect, abandonment and everything else I have been through. But, after getting some healing, I started to see things in a different light. Even now when I look back on my life, I am choosing to focus on the good and there is good in each-and-every life.

It truly is a personal choice to stay stuck, hurt, angry and broken. But it does take a strong determination to break out of that rut of ugliness and rise-up and overcome all that which we have gone through. It is so worth getting out of! You need to rise out of your situation and become the warrior that you were created to be.

One thing we need to figure out is when we are true and loyal to ourselves, we are more able to break away from all that abuse, neglect, etc. Choosing self-care and doing what is best for ourselves and for those we are responsible for. When you are your own best friend and you have God on your side, that is truly the key!

Leaving both my ex-husband and my ex-fiancé was hard, scary and very nerve racking. But I did it even though I was scared because I had children whom I wanted to do the best for. They deserved to live without fear and be brought up without trauma. I deserved to live without these things too. So, I had to make that happen. Quite honestly, I did not ever really know from time to time if I was doing it "right". I only knew that I had to do something or anything to make their lives better.

I wanted them to see what a man should be like and how they should treat a woman. The examples I had chosen were not what I wanted them to see. I was not comfortable with knowing that they would treat other women the way that I had been treated by the exes. I was not going to have that on my conscience. I am very grateful that I saw the signs of abuse and did not marry my fiance. Again, abuse comes in many forms and often it is hard to see at first.

Once again, most of the stuff that I learned were the things that I did not want to become. Self-help books, counseling and classes made this desire a reality. We live in a digital world where all these things can be found online. Here you are reading a book about this. Give yourself a pat on the back for trying to better yourself. Imagine an ideal life, what do you want your children's lives to be? My main motivation was to be a better parent than my parents were to me. I wanted my children to have a better childhood than I had. I wanted to be different then what I had been shown and knew.

I honestly felt betrayed by my parents for their lack of parenting. Back when my parents were young, they did not have the advantages that we do now such as the internet, etc. I believe that my dad always tried to be a better parent. My mom had to be a parent to her younger siblings because of my grandmother's depression and I believe that she was just "parented out" by the time that we came along.

---

Matthew 26:16 - "And from that time he sought opportunity to betray him."

---

# 22

*Helping out*

*"Condemn none: if you can stretch out a helping
hand, do so. If you cannot, fold your hands, bless your
brothers, and let them go their own way."*

SWAMI VIVEKANANDA

OVER THE YEARS, BOTH MY first husband and current husband and I
have had many people live with us. This has had disastrous results.
Many friendships and even family relationships have gone by the way-side
due to unclear expectations, lack of conversations on boundaries, and what
we really were trying to do.

Our goals were to share our home until they had saved up enough money
to get their own place. Sadly, we have not always clearly communicated
this and we were left feeling used and abused.

Another aspect of that is me being an empath. An empath is, "Highly
attuned to another person's moods, good and bad. They feel everything,
sometimes to an extreme. They take on negatively such as anger and
anxiety, which can be exhausting for them." (www.psychologytoday.
com>blog>emotional -freedom.)

I revert internally to protect myself. It is a bad place to be and go. I
never should have had to do this to protect myself, and this makes me
feel used and abused. But again, I will continue to help, while learning

of my needs, and how to protect myself and these relationships along the way. I believe that many people want a "hand out" instead of a "hand up". This is sad because I know the value of hard work to accomplish goals and dreams and making them a reality. We can have heightened self esteem when we choose to work for what we want in life rather than by being handed it. Presently, I go live every day on Facebook to encourage, support and lift up others, especially women. When you are broken you often feel like you do not deserve friendship, love, or even to enjoy a quality life. I was limiting my success, I was sabotaging my life. Out of that brokenness, I was believing that I was not worthy of that new home, that next step up, etc. I am currently trying to get people to step out of their brokenness, woundedness and allow them to see that they do have a choice in accepting the reality of their present belief or current situation. Often, we are the culprit that limits and sabotages the situation.

Many times, I would want a new home for our family. It would end up getting sabotaged because I did not believe that I was worthy of having that home. It would be my dream home at the time. I would end up being hurt, discouraged and frustrated. I would often say, "Why did Suzie get that cute little house and I can never get it?" Most of the time, at this time, we lived in condemned homes that the landlord would rent to us under the table for $75. When my ex-husband did not pay the rent, the landlord "suggested" that there was "another way" to "take care" of the past due rent for which I promptly slammed the door in his face. One time I actually had to slam the door on his toe as he was pushing on the door. I felt bad for hitting his shoe, but not badly enough to let him in. My heart was racing and fear had set in for what he had meant to do and I was disgusted by his behavior. He was actually known as a slumlord and I had first hand knowledge of his reputation. After this I wouldn't answer or open the door whenever he came around

---

Matthew 25:35- 40 - "For I was hungry, and you gave me meat: I was thirsty, and you gave me drink: I was a stranger, and you took me in: Naked and you clothed me: I wa sick, and you visited me: I was in prison, and you came to see me. Then shall the righteous answer him, saying, Lord, when saw you hungry, and fed you? or thirsty, and gave you drink? When I saw a stranger, and took you in? or naked, and clothed you? Or when you were sick, or in prison, and came unto you? And the King shall answer and say unto them, Verily I say unto you, in as much as ye have done this unto one of the least of these my brethren, ye have done it unto me."

---

# 23

## *"Keep on Keeping on"*

*"Yes, I do strive to be someone young women can look up to."*

CHYLER LEIGH

I WANT TO ADDRESS SOMETHING THAT might offend some people. I do not look at myself as a hero. I simply made a choice not to look the other way, ignore or believe that someone else would fix an issue. I chose to do something that I felt was in my power and it was something that I wished someone else would have done for me as a child. I was suffering through that same torture as a child. I decided to be different, strong, resilient and brave. I have never been sorry I did it, nor will I ever be.

During most of my younger years I was scared out of my wits and flying by the seat of my pants. A lot of people called my bravery foolish and unwise. But I am a queen who knew that there was better out there. So, I straightened my crown, be it paper or whatever and proceeded. That does not mean I didn't fall, I did, but it's ok to stop and take time to heal, rest and return to your quest.

Don't camp or live-in misery, pain or abuse. Until you clean up those wounds inside you, you will be triggered, reactive, upset, offended and hurt, a lot! Until you deal with the pain, you will be spewing your putrid volcanic lava out every time you open your mouth. This will result in nothing healthy or good and you probably are lonely and tired of everyone steering clear of you and no longer asking how you are!

We all want to be someone others can look up to and in order to do that we need to be healed. Honestly, to be wanted and needed is life's greatest joy and one of my hugest needs. I want and need to know that I mattered to someone. We cannot do that if we ourselves are broken and hurting those we love.

Recently I experienced some problems with my daily Facebook live videos. I have been getting "booted" off up to eight times a day. When I went in to talk to the girls that are the most active in the group I was hearing, "Oh no, you have to go live! We need you! We count on you going live daily to encourage and support us!" It was a huge eye-opening experience for me realizing that I am supporting and encouraging them and that I am needed. I kind of felt like Glinda the good witch from The Wizard of Oz when she said to Dorothy, "You have always had the power within you (to go back home)". You have the power within you to make the difference in other people's lives. They (the people in your circle of influence), the power within them to accept and receive the gift of your wisdom and to choose to act on it. But...they need to make the choice to help themselves.

The decision to be someone people can look up to is no easy feat. Honestly, it is hard. There will be haters, naysayers and people spewing lies about you. What they say about you is really none of your business. They are behind you for a reason. Keep on moving forward, growing, learning and doing your best. That is and should always be your focus.

There is a big difference between your reputation and your integrity. They may sully your reputation, but your integrity is what you do when no one else is around! It doesn't matter what they say, they can't change it because it depends upon what you do that no one can see. Just "keep on keeping on" and do not let their lies change a thing about you. This is what I have kept on doing. This is hard, but it can be done when you focus on YOU! While you are pursuing your healing, working on YOU, YOU have no time to worry about what others are doing. Truly, it's enough to keep you so busy, focusing on you, your healing, your future, your growth. That's the key to how you develop that resilience, keep the fire burning bright and be laser focused on you and you alone. Moving forward, keep on keeping on your path to enlightenment, healing and inner peace. You deserve this so believe it and receive it. More than that, work towards it, make small plans, commit to it, and see the changes happen. It truly is that easy. Small steps and goals, devotion to you, a better life and a better future. You've got this!

---

Genesis 26:13 - "And the man waxed great, and went forward, and grew until he became very great."

---

# 24

⌐∙⫟∙⌐

*Forgiveness*

*"Forgiveness does not change the past,
but it does enlarge the future."*

---

PAUL BOOSE

I HAVE STRUGGLED MOST OF MY life to attain forgiveness. To grant it to others, let go of bitterness, hatred and anger. After all, it is so hard to do when you are still dealing with the very things you are trying to forgive them for. Many times, we misunderstand what forgiveness is truly about. According to the Bible in Matthew Chapter 6:9-15 - "To forgive another means to cancel the debt of what is owed in order to provide a door of opportunity for repentance and restoration of the broken relationship."

In the book *The Wounded Heart* by Dr. Dan B. Allender I found a few sentences that helped me so much: "Forgiveness can be defined in terms of three components; {1} a hunger for restoration; [2] bold love and {3} revoked revenge. The process of change involves at least three things: Honesty- an open heart that acknowledges the damage of victimization and reactive self-protection: Repentance - a humble heart that enters the damage we have done to ourselves, others and the LORD: and Bold Love - a grateful heart that pursues passionate relationship with others."

"The sequence from honesty to repentance makes clear that an abused person does not need forgiveness for having experienced powerlessness, betrayal or ambivalence: she needs forgiveness for turning her soul against life with little thought of serving the deepest well-being of others. Honesty opens the heart to the battle and repentance softens the ravages of the past abuse. But more is required if life is to be deeply restored. Honesty and repentance are preconditions for life. But love sets the soul free to soar through the damage of the past and the unrequited passion of the present. The sweet fragrance of forgiveness in the energy that propels the damaged man or woman toward the freedom of love." Again, this is found in the book, *The Wounded Heart* by Dr. Dan B. Allender.

Forgiving my mother and George has been my hardest hurdle ever. They both have hurt me so much. Commonly I am just getting over one thing and another hurt happens that I need to process. It seems to be a continual cycle of frustration, making it difficult to forgive.

In processing my "mother wound", I decided that yelling, screaming, guilting and shaming her would not repair the past. Instead, as she continued her downhill decline in health, I promised God and George that I would not do anything to further the bad relationship. Instead, we were there for her, helping, listening, getting her the things she needed and honoring her as my mother (even though I felt she had not been good to me). You see, that was my karma. I did not want to have any negative karma or have this come back on me as part of my end-of-life conversation when I met God for my final review. That, I am in control of. I honored her as the word of God said to. This is between me and my God.

Forgiveness is not easy, as a matter of fact it is hard. But it sets us free, even when we believe that the person who offended, hurt and used/abused us should be the one affected, we are. I am currently reading a book and it's companion workbook by Lisa Terkeurst called, *Forgiving What You can't Forget*. It is so refreshing that she states, "Whether this was an event or a collection of hurt that built over time because someone wasn't who they were supposed to be, didn't do what they were supposed to do, or didn't protect you like they should have protected you. Your heartbreak deserves a safe place to be processed. Whoever 'they' are in your story, their actions hurt you, took from you and set off a chain of events still greatly affecting you and that was wrong."

This affected me greatly. I have not heard since counseling that I AM entitled to my feelings, just as you are. Most people don't want to hear how we feel about what they did to us. They wiggle away, squirm and balk at it, all the while making excuses. I don't know about you, but excuses make me very angry. Excuses make me feel even more angry than usual for what they did to me. Are you feeling me here? So where do we go from here? Again, we are only responsible for OUR actions, reactions and choices. We cannot make anyone change but ourselves. We need to move forward, letting go of what's behind us without the weight of bitterness, resentment, anger and unforgiveness. This may seem a monstrous step to take on. But, slowly and surely we CAN do it. That is our duty to ourselves, our healing and future.

---

1 Kings 8:50 - "And forgive thy people that have sinned against thee, and all their transgressions wherein they have transgressed against thee and give them compassion before them who carried them captive, that they may have compassion on them."

---

# 25

## Beauty in the Brokenness, Purpose in the Pain, Light in the Darkness

*"When we recall the past, we usually find that it is
the simplest things - not the great occasions - that in
retrospect give off the greatest glow of happiness."*

BOB HOPE

NOW KNOW THE INNER VOICE to be the Holy Spirit. I know Jesus is the
reason I am alive and as strong as I am today! I attribute that to my
aunt, who was my Sunday school teacher at the Baptist church we attended
when I was a child.

All my life all I ever wanted was to be loved. I often sought this in men,
family and friends when I have always had it in Jesus.

I have strived to have a home to feel safe in. It is the people who often
make it unsafe.

I have the heart of a warrior. I am short but fierce. My daddy used
to say dynamite comes in small sticks. This is so true! However, I have
mastered my temper, unless my children, my home or I am threatened
then look out! If this happens, beware, the momma bear comes out of the
cave with paws flying!

All I know is, here I am at fifty-seven and have written a book and have shared what I have learned to help people make it through this thing called life.

I have a mission. Some days I am not even sure what it is! Again, my sense of humor plays a huge part in this. My mission is to utilize the experiences that I have overcome and share, from the bottom of my heart, as best as I can how I have accomplished this.

By sharing my story, I know that you can have terrible stuff happen to you, but you can still have a good and wonderful life. I know! I have been down this road. Like many of you, I am bruised, wounded and broken by the bad choices of others and my own mistakes.

So many times, we are looking for love in all the wrong places, putting ourselves in bad and dangerous situations.

Humor input, there is a song about that by Johnnie Lee called "Looking for Love".

> *I was lookin' for love in all the wrong places*
> *Looking for love in too many faces*
> *Searchin' their eyes*
> *Looking for traces*
> *Of what I'm dreaming of*
> *Hoping to find a friend and a lover*
> *I'll bless the day I discover*
> *Another heart lookin' for love*

We end up putting up with more junk than we ever deserve. All in the name of love and being wanted, chosen and "special".

What women really need is to believe in themselves and to find self-esteem, and worthiness from the inside out. When we do this, we are more capable of finding a relationship that is healthy. With a healthy self-esteem, we will no longer choose partners based on our unmet needs, but upon sound self-beliefs.

Women grow up watching movies such as Cinderella, Snow White, Sleeping Beauty, where a charming prince on a white horse comes out of the forest to save us. We really need to understand that we can be ferocious like Mulan and Moana and be "warrior like" and save the day!

All my life I have struggled to meet other people's expectations, to be what other people wanted me to be,but then I did not like who I became. I would look in the mirror at the "real" me and this was totally different than others expectations. I could never be what they wanted me to be. It was impossible because I found out that I was not happy with what I saw in the mirror, even more so what I felt like inside. As I sit here before the computer, monitor and keyboard typing out all that my mind is spewing out. I am amazed at all the information that I have gleaned, grown through and worked hard to learn throughout my life. Honestly, I often wonder and am amazed at the stuff that I know simply by living life, reading self help and psychology books. But mostly though, my big heart and my desire to truly leave the people in life that I encounter and the world a little better as a result of my presence.

When I chose to be true to myself, the woman I saw looking back at me was brave, fierce and flying free! She is now unconfined by any expectations from society, family and friends. Being brave and true to you, is the most courageous thing you could ever do for yourself. It will bring about the most rewarding feeling and freedom.

Matthew 5:15 - "Neither do men light a candle, and put it under a bushel, but on a candlestick; and it giveth light unto all that are in the house."

# 26

## *"What If ...?"*

*"I'm always wondering about the what If's? about the road not taken."*

JENNY HAM

WHAT IF WE EXPERIENCE PAIN, trauma, blame, shame and hurt feelings and these experiences crack our lenses (eyeglasses) causing us to look through the hurts in every situation. The hurts color every situation we are in. The lenses are often foggy, scratched and unclean. When we are looking through these foggy lenses, it distorts things due to our woundedness.

We must feel those feelings and heal those hurts in order to see correctly. Which is why I highly recommend the book *The Wounded Heart* and its companion workbook by Dr. Dan B. Allender.

There once was a situation where a lady posted something that I disagreed with on social media. When we encounter a difficult conversation and we are wounded, we are more likely to become offended by things that are said when we are broken.

Instead of becoming offended, because I have gotten healed, I was able to see past the statement to the pain that she was sharing. I saw the statement, but I did not need to rise-up and become defensive or attack her. I was able to reach out and extend grace and mercy for her pain. Had I been broken, I probably would have defended myself against her beliefs wounding her further. I did not want to cause her more pain than she had already encountered. I was able to add support and encouragement rather than add to her suffering.

What if it is the starting point for healing? What if we embrace, accept and feel every one of the wounds hurts and situations? What If we make friends with it, see past the pain and use it as fuel for our future in a way that enables us to grow? What if we choose to use what we have encountered to help others through it as well? Then we would become life changers! Yes! Again, I will recommend the book by Dr. Dan B. Allender, the book and its workbook.

I know and fully understand that looking into our hurts, pain and wounds is difficult. BUT again, what if we utilize the opportunity to become healed, whole and completely free from the triggers, anxiety and fears that have traumatized and will continue to re-traumatized us? What if there is a whole new life out there that is so incredibly beautiful? Can you imagine that? What if you can be part of the solution, instead of the problem. What if you could help someone through what you have been through. The possibilities are endless, really!

I read a lot of books, went to counseling and attended many classes to get here. I sought healing with every fiber in my being. I just knew that I had to do better than my parents had done, for me, our children and my future self. For the life I knew I wanted, because I wanted to be healed, whole and happy. Happiness is not elusive, it just takes a decision to work on it, pursue it and allow yourself to have it! It is an inside job! No one else is responsible for making you happy. Not your husband, your children or your parents, family or friends. If you are not happy inside, NOTHING external will ever fill that need, desire or wish. Stop assuming that if you get that car, job or whatever you have your heart set on that you are going to be happy. It is a farce, a lie and too many people do this to their detriment. Again, happiness is an inside job. Don't assign anyone other than yourself to this detail.

There is so much healing out there to be had. Go get it! Then ask yourself, "What if?" and see what the possibilities are! Be open to those possibilities and believe that they are for YOU!

Romans 3:3 - "For what if some did not believe? shall their unbelief make the faith of God without effect?"

# 27

⁊⁊

*Surviving to Thriving*

*"No one can tell what goes on in between the person you were and the person you become. No one can chart that blue and lonely section of hell. There are no maps of the change. You must come out the other side."*

STEVEN KING, THE STAND

MY MISSION IN LIFE IS not to merely survive, but to thrive, and to do so with some passion, compassion, humor and style.

There is a meme that says: "When you can talk about your trauma without crying, that's healing!" How many of us can talk about it without crying? I can! That is with much healing, purposeful healing. I went after it on purpose. In order to make sure my future was happy and bright. Not to say that pain, heartache and trauma would never touch me, they do, but I have a completely different attitude about each-and-every moment now.

I have a different perspective. I am looking through life with a different set of eyes, lenses if you will. Knowing that each-and-every moment gives us memories, new opportunities, chances, gifts of growth, learning and an ability to add new depths of feelings and an awareness of ourselves. It is an amazing awakening. Each-and-every trial gives us new insight into ourselves and the talents and abilities that we possess.

It is like a tea bag. We have no idea what it has inside until we add hot water. Think about that! We are like tea bags, we do not know what is inside until a trial, challenge or event brings this "stuff" (tea) out of us. If we are wise, we seek to know what is inside of us and fully get to know it on our own. Life will always surprise you by bringing forth more "stuff".

I liken us to rocks. Are you familiar with geodes? Geodes are a rock that has gone through immense pressure and heat. They are spherical rocks, in which masses of minerals and matter are secluded. Typically, these include crystals. From outside, these rocks are typically ugly, with a very uneven exterior with fissures and cracks. Sometimes there are signs of what may be on the inside. This is in the form of a ridge that appears as a welded line. Inside, the geodes contain beautiful crystals. The inside is usually covered in them.

We are in the "rock tumbler" known as life. We have no idea what we have inside of us and what will be brought forth. Life is shining us up, softening up all the points, removing impurities that we no longer need or serve us.

We need to decide to stop living as though we are barely getting by. When we decide to "turn the corner" from surviving to thriving: (1) It is a life altering moment; (2) You are no longer treading water, worried about drowning, you are in the moment, focused on choosing to make the best of every situation; (3) You begin to see the positive instead of the negative and you see your whole life and outlook shift.

I used to be so stressed out. I was always so busy planning and trying to control how things would go as a way of protecting myself and those I love that I didn't really ever give myself a chance to enjoy life. Now I am pretty chill, Loving life and fully enjoying every minute I can squeeze out of it. Making memories, building relationships and helping wherever I can. Life is so joyful now.

As we grow, we have an opportunity to be brave, different, strong, kind, loving and forgiving. Just to be clear, once you have turned the corner, you must choose to pick up these talents and abilities, apply, utilize and share the light with the world.

---

Psalms 103:20 - "Bless the LORD, ye his angels, that excel in strength, that do his commandments, hearkening unto the voice of his word."

---

# 28

*~·⚜·~*

# *Acceptance - The Silent Killer*

*"Understanding is the first step to acceptance and
only with acceptance can there be healing."*

---

UNKNOWN

I AM IN COMPLETE ACCEPTANCE OF everything, yes, everything that has happened to me. I have made it my friend instead of my foe. I have graciously accepted it, all of it. Why do you ask? Because fighting with something is not the way we want to spend our time. It is a fact that it happened. Let us accept it, embrace it, play well with it and make good come from it.

Now, I am not saying I liked or even loved any of it. But again, what you spend your time on is what rules your life, mind and heart. So, I have chosen this path primarily because it is so good for my soul. Yes, it is also good for your soul. Why again you ask? Because if you heal from all your wounds you can then move on to utilizing your experiences in helping others as well. You will no longer be ruled by this pain, fear and a past that haunts you.

Ignoring it is not the way to heal from it. No, healing never comes about if you hide from it, ignore it, or put away your trauma. It is in there secretly hurting you from the inside out. It can affect your vision, attitude, emotions and life in general. Truly, it affects every area and aspect of your life. Physically, mentally, emotionally and even sexually. After all, had I not been through all of what I went through, I would not have had all the layers knocked, sanded and rubbed off of me to expose all of the kindness, understanding and patience that I now possess. This helps me to grow, learn and change.

We need those "sandpaper" people, to trigger and expose those raw sensitive nerves inside so we can be aware, work on, learn, grow and continue to heal. This rough road that I have traveled has allowed me to become who I am and for that I am so thankful!

I look at every situation in my life and use this analogy. If you are building a brick pathway and come across bricks {memories, feelings or emotions} that are unfavorable to you, but you don't have any to replace them with, you discard that brick leaving a hole where that brick should be. What then happens we have a weak spot, a place where the bricks have no support and will eventually sink, tip or move. This makes the pathway treacherous, causing a tripping hazard and sinkholes for yourself and others. So, with that analogy in mind, we must keep every brick, also known as memory, feeling or emotion. We must accept, embrace and utilize every brick in order to make our pathway strong, level, safe and an enjoyable place to walk.

If you keep the painful memories, situations, events inside of you, the poison will overrun your system. It will physically, mentally, emotionally and even sexually affect you. It can bring triggers. It can cause relationships to fray. It poisons you from the inside out. It can mess up every part of your life. It can cause you to be offended by things that normally would not bother someone who is healed.

When you are hurt, you are constantly seeking approval from others. If you find that you are not accepted in a crowd, a lot of times this is a result of being wounded and you are picking up feelings that may not be real. You may be taking offense to things that were not directed towards you. Because of the wounding, you are going to see it that way. Once again, this is where the broken lenses come into play, a normal statement that would have been said in general, would be taken by you as offensive if you are unhealed. Whereas, when we are healed, we have the ability to choose not to become offended.

Let's imagine my life as a path out of bricks and I decide that this brick is unacceptable. These bricks might represent sexual abuse, rape, mental, physical and emotional abuse. You deem one of these bricks as unacceptable to use in your path and you throw it away. But you do not have any bricks to replace that, so you will have a hole where that brick should have been. Now when you are walking along that path, you have these holes. These holes are going to become pitfalls, tripping hazards and plain dangerous. By accepting these things that have happened to us and making them our friends (instead of our foes), we can utilize these "bricks" in our lives. They can become testimonies of overcoming situations and I have found that I have been able to help others because I have accepted them.

It has been rewarding to see the pain that I have gone through helping others. One day, God said to me that I needed to go live and tell my story on a social media platform. I currently have been going live and telling my story for well over 750 days! Here I am writing a book sharing how I have overcome the trauma that I have been through. These are some of the ways that we can get our story out there to help others so that they know that they are not alone. I believe that being alone is one of the worst feelings.

Just being able to be a light to others, shine brightly like a beacon, and send out that life preserver has so many rewards. We have the choice to become bitter or better. Just like a lighthouse, they stand tall, always shining their beacon. Every single lighthouse in the world has a different horn or sound and visual appearance. The sound is designated for the times when no sight is available due to inclimate weather.

There is an audible notice of which area you are approaching.

Like the lighthouses, we each have our own individual sound and we are meant to use this to help others get "on course" and guide them in the right direction. This support has made a night and day difference in my life. There have been many beacons along my path. Once you share your light with other people, it sets about a domino effect. When you give to other people, you get feelings of joy and happiness along the journey.

There is a saying a friend shared with me and it is so appropriate for right now.

### *Our Greatest Fear —Marianne Williamson*

*Our deepest fear is not that we are inadequate.*
*Our deepest fear is that we are powerful beyond measure.*
*It is our light not our darkness that most frightens us.*
*We ask ourselves, who am I to be brilliant, gorgeous,*
*talented and fabulous?*

*Actually, who are you not to be?*
*You are a child of God.*
*Your playing small does not serve the world.*
*There's nothing enlightened about shrinking so that other*
*people won't feel insecure around you.*

*We were born to make manifest the glory of*
*God that is within us.*

*It's not just in some of us; it's in everyone.*
*And as we let our own light shine,*
*we unconsciously give other people*
*permission to do the same.*

*As we are liberated from our own fear,*
*Our presence automatically liberates others.*

*—Marianne Williamson*

---

Romans 12:2 - And be not conformed to this world: but
be ye transformed by the renewing of your mind, that ye
may prove what is that good, and acceptable, and perfect,
will of God.

---

# 29

*What Helped Me*

*"Take care not to listen to anyone who tells you
what you can and can't be in life."*

MEG MEDINA

HONESTLY, THERE ARE SO MANY things that have helped over the course of my fifty-seven years, and to this day still help!

1.  Counseling - I say this with caution, because you need to make sure that you find someone that is a good fit. Make sure you are feeling heard, understood and that it is apparent in the process of healing. Also make sure that you are seeing healing coming from these appointments. It is normal to cry, but not all the time. Healing and crying kind of go hand in hand. When it was the right fit for me, I was crying but more happy tears as we were moving through the mess, there was healing, and it was so beautiful!

2.  Journaling - I journal every single day. It is an excellent way to get stuff out, for you to look at and really see if it's what you have made it out to be. So many times, we blow situations up in our minds and make them so much worse than they really are. When we get these events out and really examine them from another

perspective. Maybe you were angry when it happened and now you are calm. It really makes a difference. Journaling gives you an opportunity to reflect on life.

3.  Writing it out - Again as in journaling, writing it out gives you the same opportunities to reflect, see how you handled the situation, event or problem. You can also use this to communicate. When I was younger, I had a difficult time saying emotionally charged stuff, so i would put it on paper and share it that way. It gets your point across and does not allow for interruptions. When you write things out, if you are concerned about people reading them (privacy), write it out, then dig a hole in your backyard, tear the page into tiny pieces, put it in the hole, add some cooking grease and light it on fire. It is a way to release the feelings without having your safety be threatened. These writings can also become poetry.

4.  Talking with friends - This was my saving grace. This is another way of getting these feelings out. Sometimes you can see things from a different perspective. Sometimes your friends are "on your side" sometimes they are not. But I absolutely loved having time to talk and get stuff out or vent if I needed to and then the problem does not often seem as bad as it really did in the beginning.

5.  Going to the beach (my happy place) - There is something calming and peaceful about the waves hitting the sand. The ocean, the waves, the sounds, the smells. Feeling the warm sand under your toes and the sun on your skin. What is your happy place?

6.  My dogs - Their never-ending love and acceptance has helped so much!

7.  Music - Music has been a therapy for me. I would hear a song that would give me the words that would describe exactly how I felt. It is like music understood me. It is a sense of support, encouragement. I would think, "Wow, that is what I should do." It is extremely therapeutic for me and it still is.

There are so many songs through the years that have helped me as it has been my sole sense of comfort, it has allowed me the words for how I was feeling. These words were not taken lightly. Again, so many songs have literally resonated in my very soul. I could post hundreds upon thousands of them that have touched me, that I may or may not have played until I literally worried that I would play the groove off the record, wear out the tape cassette or CD. But I feel so blessed to have had them guiding me, leading me upon my path, assisting me in my feelings and showing me the way.

"Worn", Tenth Avenue North. This song is like a milestone. Now that I have picked myself back up and no longer feel worn and tired, like I have lost my way, this song is a reminder of how far I have come. What a relief to feel this way and it is refreshing to see that progress.

"Beautifully Broken", Plumb

"Scars", Cloverdayle

"Faithful God", I am they

"This is Me" soundtrack from The Greatest Showman, sung by, Keela Settle. This song has given me so much courage. "I am brave, I am bruised, I am who I'm meant to be, this is me." – from "This is Me" from *The Greatest Showman Sountrack*. I felt like my weird flag had gone up full mast when I heard it. tears of JOY slipped from my eyes. We are warriors!!!

8. Art - I have really seen an improvement in my artistic abilities since becoming healed from my trauma. I have noticed that it has been unlocking levels of my artistic abilities as I've healed. I am also more open to color, and using them together. I am getting braver and more bold, and also feeling so much more confident in my artistic abilities. Healing affects EVERY area of Your life!!

9. Collaging - At first, I didn't think that you could do art or collaging as therapy. But now know that you can do both as therapy. Oh man, this has helped more than you know, for fifteen to twenty minutes search the internet or paper magazines and find pictures that just call out to you. You may not judge why or how, just take them and save them. Then, after you have your images/words/ pictures, cut and paste them onto a board either virtually or in real life. Then really go over it. It will tell you a story! It really will! You have to operate out of your unconscious thoughts when picking the pictures. Trust that your body knows what you need in this instance. The results speak for themselves. You are in awe. It is wonderful, ridiculous and awesome.

10. Reading self-help books

- "Some books you read, some books you enjoy. But some books just swallow you up heart and soul." Joanne Harris – Hplyrikz.com.
- *Girl Wash Your Face*, Rachel Hollis
- *The Wounded Heart* Book and workbook and healing the wounded heart and workbook, Dr. Dan B. Allender
- *Beauty for Ashes*, Joyce Meyer
- *Healing the Heart of a Woman*, book and devotional, Joyce Meyer
- *You Are a Heroine*, by Susana Liller.
- The Webster's Dictionary, (yes, I said the dictionary!)
- *Unstoppable Influence*, Natasha Hazlett
- *Soul Care*, Dr. Rob Reimer
- *Lies Women Believe*, Nancy Leigh DeMoss
- *Beautiful in God's Eyes and a Woman's High Calling*, Elizabeth George
- *Boundaries*, Dr. Henry Cloud and Dr. John Townsend
- *Out of Darkness*, Stormie Omartian
- *Release Your Brilliance,*Simon T. Bailey
- *GPS My Success*, Karim R. Ellis

*Forgiving What You Can't Forget,* book and workbook, Lysa Terkeurst. This book and workbook were a gift from a very dear long time friend. the gift of knowledge and power, are immeasurable. There are so many things to share in this book, but here are a few pieces that really caught my heart. "Whether this was an event or a collection of hurt that built over time because someone wasn't who they were supposed to be, didn't do what they were supposed to do or didn't protect you like they should have protected you. Your heartbreak deserves a safe place to be processed. Whoever "they" are in your story, their actions hurt you, took from you and set off a chain of events still greatly affecting you. And that is wrong. "Your pain is real. And so is mine." So, If no one has acknowledged this with you, I will. and, this one is so lyrical and magical.

"Today is the day that you start to let go of all the frustrations and fear and fragments of half-truths and flat-out lies the enemy worked really hard to get you to believe. Sort out what's true from all that's deceiving. You don't need to tidy up your words for God. You just need to pour it all out. Open the case files and examine the proof - not to use it against others but to see it all in light of God's truth. let him reveal what you need to learn from all of this and take the lessons with you...But don't weaponize your pain against others.

God is with you. He is the judge. He is your defender - the only one who can rescue and help you. Remember; resentful proof locked inside of you never exercised justice. it never made someone repent for all they've done. it only hurt you and imprisoned you behind the label of victim. It's like sitting in debris from a demolished building, refusing to let any of it be carried away. "no" you cry. "I must hold on to this shattered glass and these broken bricks, the framing all twisted and toppled like sticks." It must be seen for what it is; evidence of an ending. But once acknowledged and cleared of harmful debris, this same place is good ground for a beautiful rebuilding.

That collected proof is not treasure, nor is it a souvenir proving that a hard place you've traveled to or your secret weapon of justice. it's debris. Though you believe it's protecting you and making your world better, it's ugly and sharp. And nothing about it is healing your heart. it's time to call it what it is and start clearing it away. You can take what's not broken from among it's piles. Not everything is awful inside your memory files.

You must empty enough so you can shift from griever to receiver. There's new to be found. the *new* healing you discover will be wonderful, but it probably won't give you answers for why all this happened. Making peace with the past doesn't mean that you'll ever be able to make sense of what happened. Good thing there's something better than answers.

To get better you don't have to know why. Why they hurt you, why they misunderstood you, why they betrayed you, why they didn't love you, project you, or stay like they should. Their reasons are multilayered with a mysterious mix of their own pain. They are dealing with their own heartbreak and their own soul wrestling. And in the end, I don't think they even know all the reasons they made the choices they did.

Knowing why is no gift at all if it never makes sense.

Maybe they loved themselves too much or much too little. Maybe their hearts were too disconnected or hard or brittle. Soft hearts don't break or eat or belittle, but broken hearts with unhealed pasts can often be found traveling wrong paths. They hurt, they sting, they say words they don't really mean. The pain they project is just an effort to protect all that feels incredibly fragile inside them.

I know, because I've been there, For both the giving of hurt and the receiving of it too.

I'm so sorry for how they hurt you.

And I don't know why they did what they did or left when they left. I'm guessing they thought you were better off without them or didn't think of you at all. they couldn't see you like you needed or love you like you pleaded. They just had to go.

But answers about why are not what you need.

Waiting for something from them holds you hostage to what the other person might ot ever be willing to give.

But if you want to move on? Heal? lay down what hurts? It's 100 percent your choice to make. The steps needed are yours to take. It's what can be yours when you feel what you feel, think what you need to think and say what needs to be said.

Healing Is yours for the taking and yours for the keeping.

Emotional healing is not so much a level to reach as it is a new way of thinking you choose.

It's admitting you might be thinking about this wrong. Is there another way? There's always another way. A better place to park. A healthy lesson to learn. A way forward and onward, a future to find. We can treasure what was and leave the rest behind. We learn the lessons that lessen the grip of pain and the impossible strain to resist what now must be accepted.

When you let the hurt go and the grudges all leave, PERSPECTIVE- a really great gift - is what you'll receive. When your perspective focuses more on what you gained in this season - the new character development,more emotional maturity, the ability to help others falling this - That's healing progress! Perspective will bring a sense of revival and an assurance of survival in your heart and mind. Don't give up, don't give in and don't get lost along the way. Persevere by pressing in and finally letting the proof all go.

The proof doesn't serve you; building a case won't heal you. holding onto the hurt will only steal from you all that's beautiful and possible for you. Let it go. entrustit to God. He knows what happened and will address it in all equal measures of mercy and justice. My friend, You can trust this and carry on with your process. your heart will heal and life will go on."

WOW, right?? That was so amazing. Talk about inspiration. This part has helped me so much!

Books are my escape. I read to be a different person, little did I know that they would allow me to heal, grow and become me, the true authentic me that I have fully accepted and embraced. They also showed me the way, guiding me onto a new path, a way to heal, change and flourish. Here I am writing a book believing that it will touch others the way several have touched me.

There are so many, *Girl Wash Your Face* by Rachel Hollis. Mostly, The Wounded Heart book and workbook together by Dr. Dan B. Allender. I highly recommend it. Even if you do it alone. Take it seriously! Do it for you! Read that book and work the workbook!

11. Trusting in that which is in me/you already - Allowing it to grow, strengthen and flourish.

Grasping my difference and loving it. Embracing it. Do not compare yourself to others. When we do this, we lessen our own beauty. We are rare, unique, special, gifted and a blessing just as and who we are. A lot of times, we seek character/physical traits that we see and covet in others. An example would be if you heard someone laugh and you wanted to mimic that laugh but you could not achieve it. You would drive yourself bonkers trying to do this. When you see someone you deem as beautiful and ask, "Why can't I look like that?" you are in a sense putting yourself down rather than see the beauty that it is within you.

Hold on to you, your diverse self. Cherish, grow, nurture, develop and then share that beauty all over like it is confetti baby!

Another thing that has helped was making and having time to figure out some stuff about myself. Finding out I am an empath was huge! An empath is a person who feels others emotions, feelings and often pain. As described by Oxford Languages: "An empath is a person with the paranormal ability to apprehend the mental or emotional state of another individual." Also, as described by Highly Sensitive Refuge: "An empath is highly aware of the emotions of those around them, to the point of feeling those emotions themselves. Empaths see the world differently than other people; they are keenly aware of others, their pain points, and what they need emotionally. But it is not just emotions.

You often feel overwhelmed by the feelings, emotions and pain swirling around us. It is often difficult to tell where all these emotions come from until you take stock, become aware or learn that you are an empath.

Then it is a matter of centering and grounding yourself in awareness of yourself, so you don't become overwhelmed and overtaken with the feelings, emotions and pain. It is also one of the scary things because you literally feel other people's feelings, turbulence and drama. It is overwhelming until you figure it out...always wading through feelings wondering where it all came from and then realizing that some of it is not even yours! It took me so long to know and understand what that meant for me and to fully grasp that concept. Now I know that if I do not relate to a feeling it is probably someone else's. Whew that is big!

Isaiah 41:6 - "They helped every one his neighbour; and every one said to his brother, Be of good courage."

# 30

*You are a Special Flavor!*

*"I'm grateful for always this moment, the now,
no matter what form it takes."*

E CKHART T OLLE

D O YOU HAVE ANY IDEA how rare, special and valuable you are? You have a purpose! All, the experiences you have gone through turns into layers, colors, all melting together to become your distinct flavor. A flavor only you have! People need that flavor. You matter, you are important, you are valuable! Yes you! Even though I do not know what you have done, it matters! You matter! I can say that to you, honestly. I don't know what you have done but then again, it doesn't matter.

It's just stuff. It can be forgiven, forgotten and made better. It really can be redeemed. I can say that to you because I am fifty-seven and have seen my mistakes, bad choices and life redeemed. YOU MATTER! I have seen God bring, "Beauty for ashes, joy for mourning and healing for my brokenness". He has been a Father to a broken little girl who did not know what a father or mother's love meant. He has become my tower of strength to someone who was deeply afraid and showed me my brave side because He was standing behind me and beside me every step of the way. I pray you realize there is hope for the hopeless and that He cares about you too!

It takes bravery to help, to open yourself up to pain and rejection in order to reach people. But it is so worth it. Our soul cries out to make a difference and if we ignore that desire, I think it cripples us inside. So many of our own choices can do the same. But we can redeem that by giving our lives to Jesus Christ. He can and will redeem all our failures, mistakes, sorrows and pain. I am here at fifty-seven years old to tell you this! He has done it in and through me. He can do it through you too if you allow him to. Will you allow him to? If this is the desire of your heart, please say this prayer with me.

Lord Jesus, I know I am a sinner. Please forgive all my sins. I know I need you in my life. I ask You now to be my Savior and Lord. Come into my heart and life and renew me from the inside out. Help me to begin a new life with you. Thank you, Jesus. In Your holy name I pray, Amen.

That is it! YAY, you did it. You have started a new journey with the best help you can ever get. Now get a Bible and read it, Then find a church. Please know that all churches are not perfect. They are made for broken people finding hope. If you do not find hope and the actual word of God spoken, keep searching. By the way, if you prayed this prayer, I AM SO PROUD OF YOU!

All my life I have felt like an oddball and I felt like I never fit in anywhere. Like a round peg in a square hole. As I have grown, I have learned that I am different, rare, special and unique. We are all this way. Unfortunately, society wants us to look, act and be the same. I can't do that! Nor should you! Because we should know how special we are and how authentically beautiful we are!

I am resilient like a little helium filled balloon. I may bumble around but I always go back up. I am irrepressibly, infectiously joyful. My artful endeavors reflect the joy I share so freely with everyone I meet. My heart has and always will be for children who have been unwanted. I have always dreamed of having a home and of having a large home with property so that I could always have room to take them in. That, and abused women and animals.

Trauma creates one of 4 types of people:

1. Victims
2. Rescuers
3. Perpetrators

Or... if you are really strong and brave...

4. Survivors! I believe I am both a rescuer and a survivor! I try to help others and myself!

Some who ask for help, think they have all the answers. Some lack the knowledge to utilize this information. Oh, how I wish I would have known this sooner. It would have saved me from beating my head against a wall for times on end.

After all that I have been through, how could I not emerge as who I am? To stay unchanged would have been a great shame! Had I not utilized all that I have learned and become, I would not have grown so wise, kind and understanding. This has become such a blessing to me and others. I believe that it is our duty to become all that we can be and bring forth and utilize all that is within us. To grow, learn, accept,

- Turn on screen reader support
- Show side panel
- embrace and love ourselves and the amazing humans we have become! It is an empowering thing.

Also, the ability to find beauty in the brokenness, purpose in the pain, and light in the darkness. I happen to think that this is how we receive and show God's light. We see these qualities emerge whenever we encounter hard times. This is heavy baggage in difficult moments. It is kind of like sandpaper to the soul.

Another thing that has helped me immensely is remembering that we can never expect a return of our (roi) investment into others. All we can do is give to the fullest extent even if we never receive anything back in return.

A diamond is formed through pressure and heat. "The formation of natural diamonds requires very high temperatures and pressures. These conditions occur in limited zones of Earth's mantle about 90 miles or more below the surface where temperatures are at least 2000 degrees Fahrenheit. The critical temperature-pressure environment for diamond formation and stability is not present globally. Instead it is thought to be present primarily in the mantle beneath the stable interior of continental plates." (How Do Diamonds Form, Geology.com)

What a beautiful analogy of life and the process we go through to become who we are meant to be.

From the book *Release Your Brilliance* by Simon T Bailey he speaks about us finding our inner brilliance and says that, "Everything we need to be brilliant is already within us." And "Brilliance is inside each and every one of us!" Brilliance is not just for the pretty people or smart people or rich people. Brilliance is available to anyone and everyone who seeks it. That includes YOU!" then this one which I think is absolutely magnificent and So true about each and every one of us! "Why all the hoopla about **YOU?** first of all, you were, and still are (and always will be) a one of a kind, priceless diamond of unlimited potential wrapped in flesh. No one else on earth has your fingerprint, Your smile, your signature or your brilliance. Your uniqueness is your human signature. Hundreds, thousands, perhaps millions of people need your giftedness. **YOU** were born to release your brilliance and leave a mark on the universe. You are supposed to be here.!" I follow and listen to Karim R Ellis and he said "you are the prescription for someone else's pain" YOU are vital to someone's health, wellness and wholeness. Your unique experiences, flavor, talents and abilities matter to someone. We are here to get steeped in life so we, much like tea bags can release our giftings, talents and abilities for someone else's benefit. we get to give and we give to get.

> **"If life were predictable, it would cease to be life, and be without flavor." - Eleanor Roosevelt**

> **"You are so busy being YOU that you have no idea how utterly unprecedented you are." -John Green, The Fault in Our Stars**

Do you know what your special flavor is? How rare, unique, amazing and beautiful you are? Yes…you! All the things that you have been through is what makes you "one of a kind" and unlike anyone else. Your flavor is a diverse epitome of your life. The combination of events of your existence. Our flavor is the circumstances that we go through, the trauma, the drama and the trials that are all rolled together to make who you are. Everything that we have gone through has brought us to this point. You are amazing. You are phenomenal. You are here and you are reading this book. So now, which path will you take? Or, will you blaze a new trail?

---

Deuteronomy 7:6 - "For thou art a holy people unto the LORD thy God: the LORD thy God hath chosen thee to be a special people unto himself, above all people that are upon the face of the earth."

---